MW01045781

*To Joe, for your enjoyment;*
*Beverly Hawkins Reyner*

# MEMOIRS
## OF A COUNTRY SCHOOLTEACHER

# MEMOIRS
## OF A COUNTRY SCHOOLTEACHER

*Beverly Haskins Reyner*

| Library of Congress Control Number: | | 2013908370 |
|---|---|---|
| ISBN: | Hardcover | 978-1-4836-3780-8 |
| | Softcover | 978-1-4836-3779-2 |
| | Ebook | 978-1-4836-3781-5 |

This book was printed in the United States of America.

Rev. date: 06/18/2013

**To order additional copies of this book, contact:**
Xlibris Corporation
1-888-795-4274
www.Xlibris.com
Orders@Xlibris.com
132015

# CONTENTS

# ACKNOWLEDGEMENTS

This book is not the sole endeavor of the author and I owe my thanks to all who have contributed to its production: my husband Freal for his patience and encouragement, my children and grandchildren for their technological assistance, friends and relatives who have provided information and jogged my memory, those who have listened to my tales and said, "You ought to write a book," and my past students, without whom there would be no story to tell.

A special thanks to Bob Betts who, with his computer acumen, helped to prepare the book for publication.

IN FOND MEMORY OF

Leo Dakens
Patricia Becker
James Long
Jerry Manning
Allen Norman
Craig Turner
Donna Dakins

# CHAPTER 1

## The Contract

THE rain had stopped, but there was no moon, and after I left the lights of the little village of Comstock Park darkness enveloped me like a shroud. The headlights of Dad's 1945 Hudson shed two weak beams down the otherwise deserted highway. I had the uneasy feeling of venturing into the unknown.

Born and raised in the city, with limited preparation and no experience, I was on my way to sign a contract that would make me the sole teacher in a one-room school with twenty-five students in kindergarten through grade eight. I was beginning to doubt that I was up to the challenge, and to question the wisdom of those who had offered me the job and invited me to the meeting that night.

That I was even considered for a teaching position was due to a severe teacher shortage in the state of Michigan. Special assemblies had been held in colleges throughout the state to enlist teachers to fill the vacancies that were certain to exist in the fall. As a student in my second year at Grand Rapids Junior College, I had not yet decided on a career, but was seriously considering social work. When the assembly was announced at our college, I decided to attend, mainly from curiosity. I had given no thought to becoming a teacher. I had been attending school for almost fourteen years, most of my life. I had no desire to spend the rest of it in a classroom.

The auditorium was less than half full with the students, mostly women, occupying the first dozen rows. They were engaged in lively conversations, seemingly anticipating whatever the program provided. I looked around for a familiar face, but saw no one I recognized. Evidently science majors were not considering teaching careers in rural schools. The chatter stopped as the college president stood to introduce the speaker of the day.

Mr. Lynn Clark, Kent County Superintendent of Schools, did not look the part. He was tall, well built; handsome in a rugged sort of way. Instead of the traditional dark suit and tie, he wore a tweed sport jacket over an open-collared yellow shirt. When he spoke, it was in a deep baritone voice. He had no trouble getting the attention of his audience.

"Ladies and gentlemen," he began, "we are facing an educational crisis in our state: a severe teacher shortage! Nowhere is the problem more serious than in our rural schools. Of the one hundred seventy-three country schools in Kent County, nearly half will be without teachers in September and hundreds of children will be displaced, unless we can find teachers willing to fill those vacancies. I am here to ask each of you to consider an accelerated program, whereby you can meet the requirements for a Limited Teacher Certificate, and begin teaching in the fall."

He described the situation graphically, and as he spoke I considered my career options. I knew that a future in social work would require at least two more years of college; and a license in that field, a masters degree. My fiancé was in the army, serving with a field maintenance company that was scheduled to leave for Japan where they would repair the equipment for troops serving in Korea. He was to be discharged in two years. "Perhaps I could teach for two years," I thought, "and save enough money to continue my education and even pay for a wedding."

As we left the assembly everyone was given a packet containing the requirements for certification and an application for participation in the program. I read the material and completed the application over lunch in the cafeteria. I had taken the first step toward an unknown future.

My attention abruptly returned to the road when an impatient driver sounded his horn as he passed. His bright lights shone on a sign ahead that read PINE ISLAND LAKE ROAD. It was just what I was looking for and afraid of missing.

I made a left turn and headed west on the narrow, two lane road that followed the Rogue River. A dense growth of trees and underbrush separated the road from the river. An eerie fog crept between the trees and crossed the road, enveloping the car in mist. Peepers were serenading with their spring mating song. Not another car, house, or any other sign of human existence was visible. I wondered if this was what it was like to travel through a jungle in Brazil or perhaps Africa; without the wild animals, I hoped. Moisture was collecting on the windshield, so I turned on the wipers and leaned forward on the oversized seat. I thought about making this trip daily for two years!

Finally the route turned away from the river and the woods, revealing farms, occasional houses, and outbuildings. In a short time I arrived at the intersection I was looking for. Fonger Road was civilization! There was a schoolhouse across from a general store, and a cluster of houses. A light over the road shone dimly through the mist. I pulled up in front of the store and, by the aid of a neon sign in the window, studied the map on the seat beside me. I had less than five miles to go!

According to my watch, I had fifteen minutes to get to the Algoma Township Grange Hall. I turned north on Fonger Road, and the lights of the intersection faded. Grange Road should be right ahead. I stopped at the first crossroad and put the Hudson into reverse until I could read a worn street sign. This was it! With a sigh of relief and some trepidation, I turned left and continued on my way, arriving at my destination with five minutes to spare.

The township hall was an unimposing, white clapboard building with a single light over the entrance. Several cars were in the drive. I parked alongside the others, and made my way to the front door. The friendly greetings and smiles I received as I entered made me feel almost at ease. The superintendent greeted me by name. "You must be Beverly Haskins," he said. "Come on in and make yourself comfortable. The teachers on your left are Lois Grooters and Suzanne White. They will be teaching at the Chalmers School, not far from Gougeburg where you will be."

Lois and Sue (as she asked to be called) greeted me warmly. We shared information about ourselves, and in so doing, Lois and I realized that we were somewhat related. My Uncle John Grooters was also her uncle; and my Uncle Ed McDonald was the uncle of her fiancé. I was beginning to feel more comfortable with the situation.

A few more people arrived, and after introductions were all around, the meeting was called to order.

The Algoma Township School Board was made up of five members. One member, Freeman Teesdale, lived in the Gougeburg district, and would act as my supervisor. He had the wholesome, outdoor look of the farmer he was, with a pleasant, quiet demeanor. I appreciated the slight smile that came my way.

Other board members were assigned teachers according to district, and time was afforded for getting acquainted. Each teacher was provided with a packet of material, including a class record book and an attendance sheet that listed the names and grades of the students she would be teaching in the fall. Superintendent Clark distributed instructions for acquiring limited teaching certificates, and encouraged us to meet the requirements for such as soon as possible.

Finally Teacher's Contracts were distributed. Each was signed by the officers of the school board. My salary would be two hundred twenty-five dollars a month. This included pay for janitor work.

It was the time of decision. I considered the benefits the contract would provide: if I met the requirements I could have a teaching position for as long as I wished; but was that what I wanted to do with my life? I pondered the question until the other prospective teachers were beginning to leave the building. Finally I came to a conclusion. The agreement was for only two years; I could handle that.

I signed the contract!

# CHAPTER 2

## The Preparation

My preparation for teaching began in January 1952 with a transfer from Grand Rapids Junior College to Calvin College, where I hoped to complete the education courses required for the Michigan Limited Teacher Certificate. I was not prepared for the difficulties I would encounter in making the change. They soon became evident.

It was cold! The temperature was in the low teens, and a brisk wind was blowing. After waiting for what was probably only minutes, but seemed like an hour, the bus going to downtown Grand Rapids from the northwest side of the city where I lived finally arrived. I boarded and enquired of the driver how I might get to Calvin College.

"You'll have to go downtown and transfer to the bus going to East Grand Rapids," was his reply. He told me where to wait and when that bus might be expected. Fifteen minutes later I arrived at the site he indicated and waited another ten for the bus to Calvin. I was calculating the time that might be required for a daily commute. By the time I arrived at the Calvin campus, I had determined that I should allow an hour each morning for the trip. This was three times the time required to get to the junior college.

Once at the college, I found the Administration Building without difficulty. The office of the Registrar was conveniently located just inside. I entered and found a warm, friendly reception; I was invited to take a seat. The gentleman was busy working on some papers on his desk, but put them aside and greeted me; inquiring as to the reason for my call. I told him that, although I was late in doing so, I hoped to register for second semester classes.

The registrar was about the age of my father, with a pleasant demeanor that made me feel at ease. He perused the transcripts I had brought along, took out a blank class schedule, and began to write. After recording my personal data, he enquired about my career goals. I told him about my plan to begin teaching in a rural school in the fall and my desire to acquire enough credit hours in education to qualify for certification.

"I'm sorry, Miss Haskins," he said. "There are only two education courses being offered this semester. I can sign you up for those, and perhaps you will be able to take others during the summer session. However, there are courses required here at Calvin that you have not completed. How would it be if I enroll you in those classes?" I assented and in so doing assumed an extremely heavy class load: two education courses (taught by a Dutch professor named Dr. Van Zeef), a Bible course, biology, and a course called social problems.

I left the registrar's office and headed for the office of the treasurer. I wondered how I would be able to pay for seventeen hours of classes. I had carried a similar load at Grand Rapids Junior College, but there the tuition was less and I had a scholarship. Also I worked part-time as an elevator operator in Steketees' Department Store, putting in extra hours during the Christmas break. I was afraid that the Calvin tuition might be beyond my reach.

The treasurer proved to be as helpful as the registrar. He understood my concern, and together we came up with a payment schedule that I thought I could handle. It would require using all my savings, and working additional hours, but it seemed to be my only option. I was determined to reach my goal.

When classes began I encountered a new set of problems:

The campus was like a foreign country to me. Most of the students were residential, living in the dorms. They conversed together about places and things that I knew nothing about. I didn't know anyone, student or faculty. I had neither time nor money to attend the events that were scheduled. I had never known such loneliness.

To add to my frustration, I found that two of my classes were continuations of the first semester. The laboratory portion of the biology class had been completed before I entered the program. Frequent references to the materials, methods, and conclusions resulting from the lab sessions left me in the dark. There was no time to reconstruct the data in the library, with which I was totally unfamiliar. The fact that the class was studying human anatomy and met just before lunch added to my misery. I had only a light breakfast seven hours earlier. The visual aids used to describe the functions of veins and arteries accentuated the stomach pangs I was already experiencing.

The Bible class, "History of the New Testament," was a study of the events and theology of the new as it related to the old. The Old Testament had been thoroughly covered during the first semester. My lack of prior knowledge was a serious handicap.

Even the education classes created confusion. When I asked the Dutch professor about handling discipline problems, his reply was "When you are teaching 'Covenant Children' there are no discipline problems."

I didn't know who these children were, and whether or not I would be teaching any. Never having heard the term before, I wondered what covenant they were under. Already having identified myself an outsider, I did not ask any more questions just then.

Later a situation arose where my sense of justice would not let me remain quiet! A student asked why the public schools could offer a wider curriculum than parochial schools. Tax dollars was the obvious answer. Professor Van Zeef however, proclaimed in his strong Dutch accent, "Da chiltren off darkness are viser in diss cheneration den da chiltren off light."

My hand shot up like a bullet! I challenged his opinion of public school personal, and informed Dr. Van Zeef and the class that there were many wonderful teachers and administrators in the public schools of Grand Rapids.

As time passed, and winter began to wane, I was beginning to adjust to my heavy schedule. Then I was struck with a new, serious problem: strep throat. It started during the week with a sore throat. I treated it with cough drops and went on with school and work. By the weekend I was weak and feverish. The doctor made a call and confirmed my mother's diagnosis. I was to remain home and in bed and, as the condition was contagious, to stay away from other people until the fever left. It was a week before I returned to class, and longer until I regained my strength.

Finally the semester came to an end. I passed my classes with the lowest gradepoint average I had ever experienced. As I left my education class, Professor Van Zeef shook my hand and said, "Miss Haskins, I haf enchoyed havink you in my class. I chust regret," he continued, "that you vill not be teaching in a Christian school."

When I asked why he felt so, he replied, "The public schools are too narrow." In my usual tactless manner I asked how he could make such a statement. (My grade for the class was already recorded.) "Most of the students on this campus," I argued, "have lived in a Dutch community, attended Christian elementary and high schools, and are now attending Calvin College, without ever meeting a Jew or anyone of another race or creed."

He paused a minute before countering, "Ah, but the public school exists only in the horizontal; the Christian school exists in the vertical too." With this he pointed Heavenward. He had the last word; but I felt assured that I had given him food for thought. As I left he promised that he would visit me in my country school.

I enrolled in two education courses that summer: Children's Literature and Teaching Reading, and Art for Elementary Teachers. I thoroughly enjoyed both, and knew that I would use what I learned in my classroom. I completed the classes by the first of August, and subsequently was awarded my first teaching certificate.

Then I confronted other matters of preparation. My father, my enthusiastic supporter, agreed with my opinion that I needed an automobile. He offered to purchase one for me and I would repay him as I was able. Knowing nothing about cars, I left the choice of vehicle entirely up to Dad, and ended up with a white 1947 Ford coupe. I was delighted with the choice.

My other concern was housing. I wanted to live in the area where I would be teaching, but had no knowledge of the Gougeburg district or how to begin my search for a place to live.

One Sunday morning after church, I was discussing my dilemma with some friends. Harold Hamilton, a leader in our congregation, overheard the conversation, and offered his assistance. Harold and his wife Hazel had been Sunday school teachers and youth directors in the church for years, and we knew each other well.

"We own some property and have relatives in that area," Harold said. "Hazel and I would be glad to take you up there, show you around and introduce you to some of the residents."

I thanked him and accepted his offer enthusiastically. We agreed to make the trip that week.

A few days later, as we traveled north, Harold pointed out tracts of land that he owned. He was in the lumber business, and purchased land that contained the trees that were most profitable. The Gougeburg area however was mostly farm land. I was surprised when he turned into a driveway and drove up a hill until he came to a big farmhouse.

"My brother-in-law lives here," He explained. "I told him that we were coming. He thinks he knows of a good family that might be interested in boarding the new schoolteacher. Also, his grandson will be attending your school this fall. I believe he will be in the kindergarten."

As we were getting out of the car, the brother-in-law arrived. He had been in the fields, as the harvest was underway. He introduced himself to me and apologized for the lack of hospitality, explaining his need to get the crops in while the weather allowed. He confirmed the fact that his grandson would be attending "my school," so I would probably see him again. He suggested that we stop to see the school, which was less than a half-mile down the road. After that he talked privately with Harold about the family that might furnish my lodging, providing their names and directions to their home. We thanked him for his help.

Our next stop was Gougeburg School. We got out of the car and looked around. The grounds were well tended, and the playground equipment in good repair, but the building was locked and the windows too high for us to see inside. There were two outbuildings behind the school. One was a storage shed; the other an outdoor toilet, which was divided into two rooms. The doors were marked "BOYS" and "GIRLS".

Finally we headed to what might be my future home. It was about a mile and a half from the school. I was strangely calm as I observed the woods and pastures along the way. When we came to the large white house with a mailbox marked "Dufort", I felt like I had found a home.

A farmer and his son came to meet us. They introduced themselves as Harry and Bob Dufort. Harry, the father, was smaller than his son; and his French ancestry was evident in his appearance. Bob was taller and of sturdier build. I figured that he must resemble his mother. Both father and son made us feel welcome.

Harry informed us that his wife and daughter were returning from a trip out west, but were expected back soon. A final decision regarding my board would have to await their return. He indicated that he expected no opposition to the arrangement, and offered to show us the room in which I might be staying.

I was delighted with what I hoped would be my quarters. The room was upstairs, in the front of the house. It was immaculate and well furnished; with a double bed, a dresser, a chair, and fair-sized closet. The room was twice as big as the one I was sharing with my sister. I told Harry that I could be very comfortable there. As we parted, he suggested that I stop back on Sunday afternoon when his wife and daughter should be home.

Harold chose a different route for the drive back to Grand Rapids. It proved to be much shorter than the one through Comstock Park. I marked the landmarks mentally, determined that this would be the direction I would go on subsequent trips to and from Algoma Township.

As we travelled we discussed all that had occurred that day: we had surveyed the Algoma area, had a view of the Gougeburg School, found a possible place for me to live, and met some wonderful people. I realized how much Harold and Hazel had done for me. I would be forever thankful.

# CHAPTER 3

## Getting Settled

Sunday in Grand Rapids in 1952 was the Sabbath, the day of rest. At least that was true for the majority of the population. Stores and businesses, factories and even some gas stations were closed for the day. The "day of rest," however, was not shared by everyone in town. Many women, my own mother included, labored in the kitchen to prepare the main meal of the week, one that provided leftovers for several days. It was a labor of love for her family and any guests we may have brought home from church for the feast. It was the one time when the family of seven was together and events of the week were shared. We had learned as children to remain at the table until the meal was over and we had been excused. My visit to the Dufort farm, and the introduction to the women of that family, had to wait until dinner was over.

It was mid-afternoon before I was able to get away. Before leaving I checked my appearance carefully. I wanted to make a good impression on the Dufort women. I realized that I had been taking for granted their acceptance of me as a tenant. The men had been so encouraging; but Mr. Dufort had said that the decision would be made by his wife. Where would I live if she said "no"? Would I have to make the round trip from Grand Rapids every day? School would start in a week. There was no time to search for other lodging.

By taking the shortcut the Hamiltons had shown me I arrived at the Dufort farm in less than an hour, and was encouraged to see the whole family come out to the driveway to meet me. Harry gave me a friendly greeting, and showed me where I might park my car, and Bob offered a hearty "hello"; but it was Ellen, the lady of the house, who made me feel most welcome. She might have appeared the typical farm wife, but she had a radiant smile that made her beautiful.

"So this is our new little schoolteacher," she said. "You have already met my husband Harry and my son Bob, and this is my daughter Lorraine; we call her Rainey for short. You can call me Ellen."

Lorraine was an attractive young lady, who with her dark hair and eyes and her slim build was definitely her father's child. I could tell by her demeanor that she had reservations about my presence in her home. She offered a polite smile however, before asking a few pointed questions; like whether I would be going home for weekends and holidays. My affirmative answer seemed to her satisfaction. I hoped we could overcome whatever barriers existed and become friends soon.

"Come on in, and let me show you around the house," said Ellen as she led the way up a few stairs and through a door that opened onto an enclosed porch. "This is where we leave our boots in the winter and the men leave their barn clothes before coming into the house."

A door off the porch led into the kitchen, and just inside, easily accessible to the farmyard, was the bathroom. It, like the rest of the house, was immaculate.

"We eat breakfast and lunch in the kitchen, but have our evening meal in here," Ellen continued, as she led me into a large, attractive, formal dining room.

There were two other rooms on the main floor; a large, comfortable appearing living room, and the master bedroom. An open stairway led upstairs to three more bedrooms. Bob and Lorraine had rooms on the west side of the house. Mine would be on the east. The arrangement was perfect. I expected to spend my evenings in my room; preparing my lessons, correcting papers, and writing to my fiance', Louis, who was in the army. In this room I would have privacy and would not be intruding on the activities of the family.

Back in the kitchen, Ellen made me an offer I couldn't refuse. In addition to a very comfortable room, I would receive three meals a day; one a sack lunch for a meal at school. When I left for weekends, if I put the linens at the foot of my bed, they would be laundered and replaced before I returned. All this she offered for fifteen dollars a week! I thanked her and gratefully accepted.

As I said goodbye to Ellen, Harry, Bob, and Lorraine, with the promise to be back the following week, I felt that these good people might become a second family to me.

Returning to the city, I thought of all that had occurred since I attended that assembly at the junior college less than ten months before. I had completed the requirements for certification, obtained a car of my own, and secured a safe, comfortable place to live.

Now only one task remained. I needed to spend time alone in my schoolhouse, getting acquainted with the furnishings and resources that were already there, and adding some of my own. Upon getting home I contacted my supervisor, Mr. Teesdale, and arranged to meet him at the school in the morning.

The following day dawned bright and clear, with not a cloud in the sky. I placed a small box containing my contributions to the school on the back seat and climbed into my little Ford coupe for the now familiar trip to Algoma Township. It was early, so I decided to take the long route through Comstock Park.

What a change from when I last traveled this way! The trees along the river were beginning to change color, and the sumac had a tint of red. An occasional squirrel dashed across the road, looking for better fodder on the other side. A feeling of peace and anticipation contrasted with the anxiety I felt on that dark, lonely night in the spring.

I arrived at the school before our appointed time, and found Mr. Teesdale already there. He looked much as he had at the contract meeting in the spring, except for a deep tan, the reward of a summer of outdoor work. He wore the farmer's uniform, jeans and plaid shirt.

He greeted me at the door, and handed me a set of keys. "These are yours," he said. "Now you can come and go whenever you wish. Come on in, and I'll show you around."

The large classroom was immaculate. The floor shone and the desktops had been polished. It looked like no child had ever entered the door.

The room was arranged in the old, traditional style, with the teacher's desk centered in front of a long chalkboard and the student desks in rows facing the teacher. A low, round table surrounded by four little chairs was in the back left corner. Shelves on the back wall held books and supplies. The morning sun was shining through the east windows. It was the perfect spot for the kindergarten. The other furniture I would rearrange when Mr. Teesdale left.

We walked to the back of the room, where there was a sink with a door on either side. "That door on the right leads to the furnace room," he said. "Cleaning supplies are stored in there. This," he said, as he opened the other door, "goes to the cloak room."

He led the way into a large room that was well lit by a small window and the glass in an outside door. Rows of hooks ran along the walls. "This is where the kids hang their coats. The shelves above are for their lunch pails, hats, mittens, or whatever else they bring to school."

The outside door was opposite the one leading into the classroom. "Our bathrooms are out here." As he opened the door, I could plainly see the outhouse with the doors marked "GIRLS" and "BOYS".

"That's about it" he said as he started to leave. "If you need anything more, just feel free to call." I thanked him for his help, and was glad to see him go. I was anxious to get to work.

The first thing I did was rearrange the furniture. The teacher's desk obscured the view of the chalkboard, which I planned to use to list daily assignments and schedules. As I didn't intend to spend much time there anyway, I relegated the desk to a corner near the entrance where I could greet the children as they came in and record their attendance.

Next I arranged the student desks into groups according to grade. The smallest desks I relegated to the front of the room, nearest the teacher's desk. This would be the first grade area. The next larger desks I moved behind the first. These would serve the second grade. I continued moving desks, picturing each grade as I worked. Instead of classes moving to the front of the room for lessons, a practice that I considered time consuming and distracting, I planned to go from class to class, beginning with the kindergarten. This, I hoped, would allow me to meet with all nine classes every day.

By the time I had moved all the desks, my muscles were beginning to ache and I was feeling pretty hungry. I decided to take a break and have lunch. Aware of no restaurant nearby, I had the foresight to pack a lunch that morning when the temperature was a cool fifty degrees; but had made the mistake of leaving it in the car. As a result, my lunch was hot and soggy. I ate it anyway, washing it down with water from the sink.

The rest of the afternoon was spent perusing textbooks and teacher manuals.

Before leaving, I unpacked the box I had brought from home. I had few items to contribute, but what I had were important to me. I hung my pictures and a colorful calendar and put some children's books on the shelves in the back of the room. My treasured anthology went on the Teacher's desk, along with a brass bell that I had purchased with my last paycheck from Steketee's Department Store.

As I checked the room one last time before leaving, I was struck with the reality that, when I returned, it would be as TEACHER!

# CHAPTER 4

## Opening Day

The first day of school finally arrived. After a cold, wet holiday weekend, the sun broke through the clouds, along with the gift of a beautiful rainbow. Although I had missed the opportunity of spending the last weekend of the summer at the beach, I enjoyed the time spent with family and friends; relaxing, talking, playing table games: just being together. We were all aware that occasions like these would be rare as we went our separate ways. Now, putting nostalgia aside, I was heading, with anticipation, in a new direction on the road of life. I reached the schoolhouse an hour before the children were due to arrive. The room was just as I had left it. I printed my name in big letters on the chalkboard; then sat at the desk and reviewed my plans for the day.

It was shortly after eight when I heard a car drive into the yard. The sounds of opening doors were muffled by happy children's voices. A soft feminine voice cautioned the kids to quiet down. The front door opened and an attractive young woman entered followed by four children, two boys and two girls. "Good morning," I said. "I'm Beverly Haskins, the new teacher."

The woman returned my greeting and introduced herself. "I'm Lillian Teesdale," she said, flashing a beautiful smile. "My husband has told me all about you. I'm glad to meet you. These are my boys, Tom and Ron, and my daughter, Sandy. This is my little niece Pamela. I understand you haven't taught in a country school before. Tom and Ron will be glad to help you however they can, won't you boys?"

They answered with nods and shy smiles, while the little girls looked up at me and grinned. They were telling me their ages and grades when the door opened and several more children and a few parents came into the room.

I turned to greet the new arrivals and introduced myself. As they told me their names, I realized that my student body would include several family groups: three Manning boys, three Holden girls, four Dakin children, and Jim and Christine Long. How would the interrelationships effect behavior and learning? I guessed I would soon find out.

Children continued to arrive until eight-thirty when school was scheduled to begin. The parents left, chatting with one another as they went. I rang my bell, announcing the start of the new school year.

As I looked around the room, I was impressed with how attractive and alert the children appeared. "It must be the country living that puts the color in their cheeks and sparkle in their eyes," I thought.

"I am Miss Haskins," I said. "My name is on the board. Now I would like each of you to tell me your name and what grade you are in. We will begin with the kindergarten."

One by one the children stood and introduced themselves. As they did so, I marked their attendance in my record book. If necessary, I directed them to seats in their grade area. I explained my plan to go from class to class for lessons, and my reasons for doing so. Some nodded their heads in understanding or approval. Others seemed a little bewildered at all the changes. It was time to turn to something familiar.

"How do you usually begin the day?" I asked. "What do you do after the bell rings and you take your seats?"

Ruth Knox, an eighth grader, answered. "We say the 'Pledge of Allegiance to the Flag and sing 'God Bless America'. Oh yes, and sometimes the teacher reads a chapter from the Bible."

"That sounds like a good way to start," I said. "Would everyone please stand while I get the flag from the corner?"

I moved the flag into view, and turned to see the children standing at attention, right hands over their hearts. The little ones were watching the older kids to make sure they were doing it just right. I followed their lead and faced the flag. We offered the pledge and sang the song with enthusiasm.

The children took their seats, and I found a rather worn Bible on a shelf near the front of the room. I brushed some dust from the cover as I spoke. "This morning I am going to read the first chapter from the first book of the Bible. Does anyone know the name of that book?"

"Genesis," replied several of the older students in unison.

"In the beginning God created the heavens and the earth." I began, and read on until I had finished the chapter. I looked up and found the students relaxed and attentive; ready for whatever was ahead.

It was time to get to work. "Starting tomorrow and from then on, the assignments for grades four through eight will be on the chalkboard," I said, "but this morning you all have the same task: to tell how you spent your summer. Those who can write will write about it, and those who can't will draw a picture and tell me about it when I visit your class. I will help the kindergarten and first grade get started; then I will go around the room and give help to anyone who needs it. Do you have any questions?"

No one answered, but I thought I heard a quiet groan.

Three little boys and a pretty little girl were seated around the kindergarten table. Any one of them could have been a cover child for "Parents Magazine". Steven Powell had red curls and freckles over the bridge of his nose; Allen Norman was a miniature Clark Gable, with dark hair and a winning smile; Wayne Wainwright looked angelic, with blond hair, blue eyes, and rosy cheeks; and Diana Davison had was a pretty little girl with a smile that melted my heart.

None of these children had an older brother or sister in school, so everything was a new venture for them. I sat down with them, and we discussed how they felt about starting school and what they did to prepare for this first day. I told them that it was my first day of teaching, so I knew how they might feel. They thought that was kind of funny.

They took turns telling of their summer adventures and what was most fun. Then I gave them each a sheet of Manila paper and crayons, and asked them to draw a picture of that event. As I left them, the kindergarteners were working diligently on their original school creations.

I walked toward the first grade area where Sandy and Pam Teesdale were holding up their pictures, announcing that they had finished their creations and were ready to tell all about them. Christine Long gave me a sweet smile and said that she was "almost done."

One little girl sat quietly, looking down at the blank paper on her desk. She was Lorene Dakins, the youngest of the Dakins children. While the other girls told of family reunions and trips taken, Lorene continued looking down at her empty paper. When I asked about her summer, she answered, "We just stayed home."

"We can have good times at home too," I said. "I bet you and your sisters and brother have fun playing together. Is there a game you like best, or do you ever play house? Maybe you just like helping your mother."

She looked up at me and her eyes began to light up. "It's recess time now, but how would you like to stay in for a few minutes, and I'll help you get started." She gave me a nod and smile of gratitude.

I rang my bell, and announced recess time, and in a few minutes the room was empty, except for Lorene who was busy working on her picture. In no time at all she had made a pretty good sketch of her home and children running around it playing a game. I told her that it was a very good picture and I would be putting it on the bulletin board along with some others. With a happy smile, she hurried out to the playground to join the rest of the kids.

While the children were out, I gathered the finished pictures and put some puzzles on the kindergarten table. Then I went to the door and rang the bell again. Recess was over.

The children came in laughing and talking. They took turns at the drinking fountain. Evidently they had enjoyed the chance to be outdoors on such a beautiful day. In a few minutes the room was quiet and the children were looking at me expectantly.

"After morning recess we will usually have math class," I said. "This morning the kindergarten will work on the puzzles that are on their table. The first grade will write their numbers, going as high as they are able. The rest of you are to do the problems on the first page of your math book."

"This is a review of what you studied last year. Please do not help one another today. You will not receive a grade for your work; It will help me decide where you should begin this year. If you finish before lunchtime, you may get a book from the library or draw a picture of your choice. I will be checking to be sure you are on the right page. Are there any questions?"

No one responded, so I directed them to begin.

I stopped at the second grade area where Jerry Manning and Judy Turner were ready to hand me papers describing their summer adventures. I was surprised and pleased that they were able to write in complete sentences. The pictures they drew were quite graphic. I was impressed with the progress these children had made in one year.

I asked them to take out there math books. Without further instruction they had them open to the proper page, and were concentrating on the first problem. It was not the time to interrupt, so I just gave them a nod and a smile, and determined to spend more time with them as I was able.

By now the kindergarten had wearied of the puzzles. It was nearly time for them to go home, so I read a short story to them. I was just finishing when their parents arrived. The children greeted them enthusiastically, evidently pleased with their first day of school.

At noon we stopped for lunch. The children brought their meals to their desks and sat down expectantly. They informed me that they usually said a prayer before eating, which surprised and pleased me. It happened to be one I had learned as a child, so we prayed together:

"God is great. God is good. Let us thank Him for our food. By His hand we all are fed. Thank you for our daily bread."

After the prayer I took my lunch out of my desk, and ate with the children. I realized that I was hungry, and the sandwich I had made the night before from my mother's leftover roast beef, although by now a bit soggy, tasted delicious.

The children ate quickly, anxious to return to the playground. I opened some windows to let the fresh air into the classroom before going out to watch them at play. When they saw me several came over to chat, and I enjoyed the opportunity to get better acquainted.

The afternoon was spent perusing the new textbooks; introducing the spelling words and the content of the science, English, and social studies books. I went from class to class, answering questions and making sure the students were ready to begin their studies in the morning. The time passed quickly, and before I knew it, it was time for dismissal. I was pleased to see the children straighten up their desks and work areas before heading for the cloakroom to retrieve their lunch boxes. They left with friendly "goodbyes" and promises to see me tomorrow.

It was then I realized that my work was not done. I had signed a contract that included janitor work, and I hadn't the vaguest idea of what the job entailed. Through observation and study I had learned something about teaching, but Calvin College offered no courses on janitor duties.

Leo and Donna Dakins were just going out the door when I called them back. "Can you help me?" I asked. "I am to do the janitor work, and I don't know the first thing about it."

"Sure," Leo responded with a big grin. He went to the storage room and returned carrying a five gallon bucket.

"This is sweeping compound," he said. "First you move all the desks over to one side of the room. Then you scatter this over the empty floor, and let it set while you clean the chalkboard. Next you sweep it up, and move all the desks over to the clean side. You scatter compound on that side and let it set while you sweep out the cloakroom. After you sweep up the compound and move the desks back, you empty the waste basket into the burn barrel outside. That's all there is to it."

I thanked Leo for his help, and he and Donna left for their long walk home.

The directions he gave were simple, but carrying them out proved more difficult. After moving the desks once, my muscles rebelled at moving them a second time. However, I finally had the room in order with clean floors and chalkboards. The entry and cloakroom had been swept. When I carried the waste basket out to the burn barrel the sun was low in the western sky. I was more than ready to head back to the farm.

I arrived just in time to enjoy a roast beef dinner complete with a delicious dessert. There was no time to linger at the table, however. I had papers to correct, lessons to prepare, and a letter to write.

Finally my first day of teaching came to an end. Tired but contented I prepared for bed. The bed was comfortable, and I was soon sound asleep.

# CHAPTER 5

## Lessons Learned

The first week of school was spent getting established. I was learning to teach as I practiced, using methods that, though untested, seemed practicable to me. The practice of allowing students to help one another was evidently new to the children, and I had to remind them that this did not include sharing answers.

I learned from the children also. One day one of the older students who had completed her assignments asked if she might read a story to the younger children. I readily accepted her offer and soon other students volunteered to help. Most of the eighth graders were very good students, so I used their services on a regular basis. Instead of using their free time to read or participate in other activities they chose to help the "little kids", which in turn was a big help to me, allowing me to spend more time with students who needed special assistance.

The janitor work, however, still posed a problem. I was underweight; not built to move furniture. The big teacher desk was especially heavy, so I left it in place and did my best to sweep the dust from underneath and I decided that was sufficient as the desk was seldom used. Although I was slowly gaining in efficiency, I was not fond of the job which left me with sore muscles that I didn't even know I had; but I reminded myself that this was part of the contract and did my best.

On Friday afternoon, with a sense of accomplishment, I locked the schoolhouse door and headed for my home in Grand Rapids.

I approached the second week of school with confidence; looking forward to a return to "my classroom."

The weather that week was sunny and bright, with just a touch of fall in the air. I woke early one morning and, feeling invigorated, decided to walk to school, which was only a mile and a half away. Grange Road was paved, and I covered that half-mile with ease. However, Eleven Mile Road, which led to the school, was gravel. This slowed my progress, but gave me time to admire the woods on my left which were just beginning to change color.

On my right was a pasture with a herd of cows feeding on a knoll some distance away. They looked up and, seeing me, stopped eating and headed toward me. All at once they started to run, kicking up dust as they came. I had seen movies involving stampedes and began to feel more than a little anxious. Suddenly they stopped and lined up along a thin wire fence. From there they watched me until I was out of sight.

By the time I arrived at the schoolhouse I had regained my composure, but my feet were sore from the pressure of gravel on the thin leather soles of my shoes.

I was surprised to find the building unlocked and Tom and Ron Teesdale inside. Evidently their father, my supervisor, had driven them to school. They were standing at the windows, looking down the road I had just traveled.

"Where is your car?" Ron asked, looking out the windows on the other side of the room.

"It's such a beautiful day that I decided to walk to school," I replied. Then I proceeded to tell them of my encounter with the cows and my surprise at their behavior. I said that I was familiar with the cows on the Dufort farm and had been in my grandfather's barn at milking time, but never had seen cows behave like those from the knoll in that pasture.

Tom gave me my first lesson in bovine anatomy. "Miss Haskins," he said, as he looked out the window and down the road, "those aren't cows; they're steer."

I thanked him for the information and wondered how much more the children would teach me while I was being paid to instruct them.

Now the other children were arriving, so I put the episode behind me. Except for my sore feet I was able to forget it while we went on with the activities of the day.

The hours passed quickly, with the students busy at their lessons, seemingly happy with their new routine. Too soon the school day was over, and it was time for them to leave. As the last one left with a friendly "See you tomorrow," I realized how tired I felt. I sat at the teacher's desk, a place seldom used, and rested until gaining the energy for janitor work.

The work seemed exceptionally onerous, and I made slow progress. Before long the room was getting dark. I turned on the lights and glanced at the clock to see that it was almost dinner time, and I still had desks to move and a waste basket to empty. I was just coming in the back door when the front door opened and Bob Dufort walked in.

"What happened?" he asked. "We were worried about you. We thought you might have run into trouble walking home. Dinner is on the table."

"I'm all right, but I think we'd better go," I replied. "I'll tell you all about it later. I don't want to keep your folks waiting any longer."

In a few minutes we arrived back at the farm to find the family already seated at the table. I apologized for being so inconsiderate. Ellen had prepared another delicious meal, and I had kept them all waiting.

They graciously accepted my apology and agreed that, knowing I had walked to school and intended to walk home, they worried that something had happened to me.

During dinner I told them about my day, including my encounter with the cattle and the effect of gravel on my leather-soled shoes. I bemoaned the fact that I showed little if any improvement in my role of janitor.

To this Ellen replied, "You know Bev, some teachers hire students to do the janitor work for them."

I perked up at that news! How great it would be to be able to correct papers and plan lessons before leaving the schoolhouse in the afternoon. I might even have time to relax in the evenings and get better acquainted with my foster family.

"Oh, thanks for telling me, Ellen," I said. "That's wonderful news. I think I'll look into it tomorrow."

After dinner, as I went up to my room to perform my nightly chores and write another letter to my soldier, I thought, "Soon I may be able to linger at the table or help with the dishes; to feel a real part of the family, instead of just a tenant."

The following morning I was at my desk reviewing my lesson plans when I looked up to see Leo and Donna Dakins standing before me. "Good Morning," I said, giving them a warm smile.

Leo, never one to waste words, said, "Teacher, could Donna and me do the janitor work for you?"

I never did find out how they knew I was intending to hire a student janitor as I had told no one, but I could think of no better candidates for the job.

"I can pay only ten dollars a week," I said. "Would you be willing to share that amount?" They smiled and nodded in agreement.

"Would your parents agree to your taking the job?"

I was surprised at Donna's reply, "They said we could do it."

"Well then, when would you like to start?" I asked.

"How about this afternoon after school?" Leo responded.

He couldn't have given a better answer! I agreed, of course, and felt a load removed from my shoulders. I was delivered from an occupation I never hoped to resume.

That evening, with papers corrected and lesson plans complete, I offered to help Ellen and Lorraine with the dishes. This became a nightly ritual and, as we worked together, we talked about many things. Eventually we developed a bond that included me in that wonderful family.

# CHAPTER 6

## Three Visitors

Strangers seldom came to our little school, so we were surprised that fall to have three visitors.

The first arrived early in the year. School had been in session for about a week, when classes were interrupted by a knock on the front door. I went to the door and opened it, to find a young man, probably no older than myself, standing before me with a pencil and notebook in his hand. He looked me over and said, "Could I speak with the teacher, please."

I stood as erect as possible and replied in my most authoritarian voice, "I am the teacher."

Looking a little embarrassed, he went on to explain that he was a milkman, there to take orders for the half pints of milk that the kids could have at lunch or recess. He would be able to make a daily delivery if he received more than just a few orders. I took a quick poll of the children and found that no one was interested in his offer, as they had thermos bottles of their chosen beverages in their lunch buckets. I thanked the young man for stopping and went back to the class I was teaching before this brief interruption.

The second visitor came later and stayed longer. In early October I responded to another knock, and admitted an older woman whom I introduced to the children as Mrs. Thompson, an instructor from Western Michigan University. I explained that Mrs. Thompson would be spending the morning with us, to see how we did things at our school. To ease any anxiety, I added that she would be visiting other schools too. I didn't tell them that I had enrolled in a class called "Practice Teaching for Teachers" and she was my professor. I wanted her to observe a normal class environment. In truth, I was proud of the behavior of my students.

When the children went out for recess, Mrs. Thompson offered her opinion of my teaching and made a few helpful suggestions. She declared that bulletin boards were no longer used to frame student handiwork, but should be used as teaching tools. She suggested that I replace the student creations with colorful math or science lessons, claiming that this would reinforce their learning whenever the children looked at the display.

Next she asked to see my class record book. As she scanned it she observed that one student had received a "C" for the first marking period while receiving "A" for each daily assignment. I explained that the student worked very hard and was conscientious, but was performing almost two years below grade level. She advised me to give him the "A" he had earned and reluctantly I agreed to do so.

Finally she shared some information that I found extremely helpful. She offered me a copy of a magazine called *THE GRADE TEACHER*, which contained practical suggestions for enriching the curriculum through art, music, and games. I subscribed to the magazine and subsequently looked forward to each monthly issue.

Mrs. Thompson was preparing to leave just as the children were returning from recess. I hoped that she found their happy smiles and friendly goodbyes as endearing as I did.

After school, as my new janitors were cleaning the classroom, I removed the pictures and other schoolwork from the bulletin board and replaced them with brightly colored construction paper. Using twelve paper circles I was able to demonstrate multiplication and with a red paper apple cut into slices, a division problem.

The reactions of the children the following morning were not what I expected. "Why did you take down my picture?" one kindergartener asked in dismay. Another student wondered about the whereabouts of his perfect spelling paper. Other students joined the chorus until I was convinced that attractive bulletin boards displaying math and science lessons did not meet the needs of my students. By the end of the day the apple slices and colored balls were replaced with colorful pictures and compositions submitted by the children.

Our third visitor that fall, my old Calvin College professor Dr. Van Zeef, arrived one cold November morning. He was wearing a long woolen coat with a bright red scarf that accentuated his white hair and beard. With his cheeks rosy from the cold he bore a striking resemblance to pictures of old St. Nicholas.

The children stopped their work to stare and I realized that they probably had never met anyone like him. "Children, this is Dr. Van Zeef from Calvin College. He was my professor when I was preparing to become a teacher, and he promised to visit our school." Turning to my old instructor I added, "Welcome, Professor; it's good to have you with us."

He smiled at the children, and in his familiar Dutch accent replied, "Tank you for dat vorm velcome; but I don't vant to interrupt your vork. Chust go ahead vith vut you ver doink, and I vill chust make myself at home."

I took his coat and scarf and offered him the chair at the teacher's desk, explaining to his questioning look that I seldom used it. Then, after hanging his wraps on the rack next to mine, I returned to the task at hand.

During the morning I found the children casting furtive glances at the old man. When he caught them he responded with a warm smile and they usually reciprocated. When the kindergarten was dismissed for the day, the good professor decided it was time to take his [1]leave. He retrieved his warm coat and bright scarf, and said goodbye to the children. At the door he turned to me and quietly said, "Miss Haskins, your chiltren luf you."

"I know," I replied. "I love them, too."

[1] THE GRADE TEACHER THE PROFESSIONAL MAGAZINE. (1952) Darien.Connecticut Educational Publishing Corporation.

# CHAPTER 7

## A Country Halloween

The celebration of Halloween in the country was a far cry from anything I had experienced in Grand Rapids. In 1952 the holiday fell on a Saturday, so I informed the students that we would have a party on Friday afternoon and invited them to wear costumes if they wished. I envisioned an event like those held in elementary schools in the city with a few games, cookies and punch, and possibly a prize for the best costume.

The next morning a mother stopped by to tell me that it was customary at Gougeburg to have the Halloween party in the evening so that whole families could attend. She informed me that the parents would take care of everything, and my only obligation was to be there. She advised me to dress casually, as there would be a hay ride.

On Friday evening I arrived at the schoolhouse to find the room already crowded with everyone from toddlers to senior citizens. Our township bus driver, Marvin Jewell, who also delivered our school supplies, was there to drive the tractor for the hayride. I recognized several mothers who were supervising the "diving for apples" event. The desks and chairs were pushed back against the walls to allow for other games that were in progress. Some people stood around in small groups talking. Cider and doughnuts, along with some Halloween candy, were on the Kindergarten table. There was a festive mood in the room.

At approximately eight o'clock Marv Jewell announced in a loud voice that it was time to board the hay wagon for the major event of the night. I have no idea how many were on the wagon or their identities. I do know that some took delight in gently pushing the teacher off, causing me to walk or run for a short spell while I heard my little children's worried voices shouting, "Our teacher fell off the wagon." At this Marv would stop, allowing me to catch up and with the help of many hands regain a seat on board. This tomfoolery was repeated several times before the pranksters were convinced that it did not upset me in the least. We arrived back at the schoolhouse to find hot chocolate and coffee added to the refreshments on the table.

Finally the party began to wear down. Sleepy toddlers were carried out to waiting vehicles by their parents and tired school children followed in their wake. Mr. Teesdale, knowing that I had a long drive back to Grand Rapids, invited me to leave while he and others cleaned up after the night's activities.

I drove back to the farm, intending to pick up a few items and drive on to the city. I was surprised when Lorraine offered an invitation that sounded like fun. She had two ugly rubber masks that completely covered the head; one representing a female and one a male. At her suggestion we put on an oversized dress and overalls, padded our bodies with pillows, donned men's boots and gloves, and finally the ugly masks. Totally unrecognizable, we paid a visit to her brother Bob and his friend Paul Fonger who were tending Fonger's General Store.

Before knocking at the door we agreed to be absolutely silent, which meant no speaking, laughing, or any other noise. With that, Lorraine gave the door a solid knock. Paul answered and gave us a look of amazement. Before he could gain his composure to ask who we were or what we wanted, we had brushed him aside and entered the apartment behind the store.

Bob was seated on a sofa in front of a television set. On a coffee table in front of him were an open bag of potato chips and a couple cans of soda. Two armchairs completed the seating arrangement. We promptly claimed them and made ourselves comfortable.

The guys looked us over head to toe and, laughing and prodding, tried to convince us to reveal our identities. We pretended to watch the program on the TV, and occasionally looked in their directions, but didn't make a sound. This went on for over an hour when Lorraine abruptly got up and headed for the door, with me at her heals. We left as we had arrived, without saying a word.

The following morning, as I enjoyed a hearty breakfast with the family before leaving for the city, Bob amused us with a vivid description of the weird couple who had invaded the store the night before. We all pretended ignorance, but afterward I had reason to believe that he knew who the impersonators were all the time.

It was time to leave for the city, but before I got to the door, Harry stopped me and said, "Bev, I think you should drive by the schoolhouse before you head for Grand Rapids."

"What's wrong!" I responded, envisioning smoldering remains of a burned out building.

"Nothing to worry about," he replied, and the smile on his face relieved my anxiety. "Just head that way and you'll see what I'm talking about."

I took his advice and as I approached the school knew why he had directed me there. In the distance, was my schoolhouse with the outhouse towering above the roof! My amusement was coupled with concern; "how did it get up there, and how in the world was anyone going to get it down?" I decided that problem was not a part of my job description, and best left to those in the know. I felt sure that the situation had been dealt with before.

That was the case, for when I arrived for work the following Monday, the outhouse was in its customary place, the schoolroom had been cleaned, and all evidence of a country Halloween celebration had been erased.

# CHAPTER 8

## Happy Holidays

Fast on the heels of Halloween the first snowfall arrived, ushering in the holiday season. It began early one day in late November while the kindergarten class was composing a story to accompany the pictures in their pre-reading books. Steven Powell looked up from his work, and glancing out of the window exclaimed with a joyous shout, "It's snowing!"

With that announcement all work stopped and every eye in the room was fastened on the windows where the first flakes were drifting slowly to the ground. The younger children were straining to look over the high sills, so I gave them a nod and a smile, my invitation to go to the windows and watch the snowflakes as they swirled over the brown playground.

Returning to the task at hand was impossible, so I announced an early recess for the kindergarten, first, and second grades; and told the older students that they were free to go outdoors whenever they completed their assignments. Through the windows I watched the children on the playground as they danced around with their mouths open, trying to catch snowflakes on their tongues.

When they tired of the activity and felt the cold wind through their inadequate clothing, the little ones reluctantly made their way back indoors. Their cheeks were rosy and their eyes shining, as in a noisy chorus they tried to describe their adventures in the world of snow.

Realizing that a return to lessons was impossible, I provided blue construction paper and pieces of chalk with which, along with a few crayons, they were able to produce some very impressive winter pictures. Some replaced the Halloween pictures on the bulletin board, but the kindergarteners, their morning session over, proudly presented their creations to their admiring parents who had come to take them home.

By noon the entire playground was covered with a blanket of white. Most of the children ate lunch quickly; then hurried out for fun in the snow. Some lay on their backs and moved their arms and legs to make outlines of angels. Others, mostly the older boys, made snowballs and enjoyed a harmless war, with no victors or losers. Eventually all succumbed to the cold wind, and came inside to get warm and relax.

The snow continued to fall and, as the students made snowflakes from typing paper, I read them a story about a schoolgirl somewhere in the Dakotas who gave her life to save her younger brother and sister from freezing to death in a blizzard. While the children opened their math books for the last class of the day, their somber faces made me wish I had chosen a more cheerful narration.

It was still snowing when classes ended and school was dismissed, so I invited the Dakins children to remain until the janitor work was done; then I took them home in my little Ford coupe. It was a tight squeeze for the five of us, but much more comfortable than a long trek through the deepening drifts.

Most of the snow had melted by Thanksgiving, to the disappointment of the children. However, the days preceding the holiday were enlivened with special stories and lessons about Pilgrims, Indians, and other early settlers of our country. We sang Thanksgiving songs, and the little children made Indian jackets and feathered headbands out of brown paper bags while the older ones constructed turkeys from pine cones.

I was concerned that the children had acquired most of their knowledge of Indians from western movies, and thought of them as "bad guys." I was determined to change this perception, and searched for material to reinforce my teaching. I had heard that the county library had movies and projectors that teachers could borrow at no cost. On Monday evening I called to inquire of a film I might use to provide the children another view of the American Indian.

The librarian suggested a film that was recommended for children in the upper elementary grades. It's was labeled "Life in an Indian Village." I asked her to reserve it, along with a projector, and told her that I would pick them up after school the following day.

On Tuesday afternoon I helped Leo and Donna with the janitor work so I could leave for Grand Rapids as soon as possible. The county library closed at five o'clock and, never having been there, I was unsure of the shortest route to the facility. With luck, I arrived fifteen minutes before closing, in time to collect the film and get brief directions for the use of the projector.

Wednesday morning was spent completing Thanksgiving projects and class work in preparation for the long holiday weekend, and it was lunchtime when I decided to set up the projector and thread the film. With no experience and only the directions provided by the librarian, I found this no easy task. Finally, just as the children were coming in from noon recess, I was ready to show the film. I turned on the projector for a quick preview, and to my dismay saw an Indian village with a dozen little children running around stark naked. I turned off the projector, but not before the Teesdale boys and perhaps some others had a glimpse of the pictures on the screen. This film was certainly not acceptable for my elementary students! I explained to the disappointed children that it wasn't the film I intended to show, and hoped to find a more suitable one in the near future.

It wasn't long before disappointment gave way to the anticipation of the long weekend ahead, and the afternoon recess echoed with hopes and expectations for a fun-filled vacation.

School was dismissed and the children were leaving the building when Mr. Teesdale arrived with my paycheck and a request. "It's our tradition," he said, "for the children to put on a Christmas program before school closes for the holiday vacation. The event is held at night and the whole community attends. Would you be willing to plan the program and help the kids learn their parts?"

I must have looked a little dubious, for he continued, "The men will set up a stage that you can use for practice, and the Baptist minister's wife has agreed to play the piano."

"I've never conducted a Christmas program," I finally replied, "and my only experience has been church performances, but I will do my best."

The promise must have been acceptable, for he left saying, "If there is anything else we can do to help, just give me a call."

The four days of rest and recreation that I had planned just took on a new dimension. In three short weeks, filled with a myriad of holiday activities, I must prepare my students for a Christmas program for which I had no prototype.

I stopped by the farm only long enough to pack the few items I planned to use that weekend and to wish the Duforts a happy Thanksgiving. Then I headed for Grand Rapids, hoping to find the libraries still open and able to provide some material relating to children's Christmas programs.

A public library was located just a mile from my home and I decided to make that my first stop. To my dismay I was greeted by a sign in the window which read, "CLOSED FOR THE HOLIDAYS" and below, "Open on Monday 9AM to 9PM." There was no need to make the rounds of the other public libraries in town, for if one was closed the others were sure to be also. I turned the car around and headed for home.

Before opening the door I was greeted by the tantalizing aroma of my mother's homemade apple pies. They were a labor of love, prepared the day before the holiday. A huge turkey, large enough to feed our extended family, would monopolize the oven from early Thanksgiving morning until mid-afternoon when dinner was served.

I deposited my bag in the room I shared with my sister, changed my clothes, and went downstairs to the kitchen where the women were preparing for the evening meal and the feast to follow the next day. When the work was done, the family gathered around the large dining room table for a somewhat smaller but substantial meal.

As we ate supper we discussed the events of concern to each of us. I told of my agreement to prepare a Christmas program and the lack of direction or resources to do so. I mentioned my stop at the public library and the note on the door.

"Maybe the college libraries will be open on Friday," my sister Marie suggested "but they probably wouldn't offer much in the way of children's programs."

"Why don't you check with Mrs. Hamilton from the church?" my sister Betty asked. "She has been responsible for the children's Christmas program for ages. She probably has material that she would be glad to share."

Encouraged by the helpful suggestions of my sisters, I put aside my concerns and joined in the holiday festivities. We were a close knit family and whenever we gathered the conversation involved the well being of the entire clan. Our Thanksgiving celebration included, in addition to the delicious feast, an inordinate amount of chatter, table games, music, and before the day ended, plans for a Christmas celebration. It was nearly midnight before the guests left and the rest of us retired for the night.

On Friday morning I called the colleges to inquire about weekend library hours and the program materials I was seeking. I received disappointing replies to both. Because of the holiday weekend, if the libraries were open at all, the hours were limited; and the only children's material available were those used by the students enrolled in education departments.

My final hope lay with Hazel Hamilton who, along with her husband Harold, had been instrumental in introducing me to the Gougeburg community and helping me find a place to live. They had already gone out of their way for me, and I was reluctant to ask them to help again.

Hazel answered my call with a cheerful greeting, and my inquiry for suitable Christmas program material met with an enthusiastic response. "I have just what you are looking for," she said. "It is a book of Christmas ideas for Sunday school, intended for children in the primary grades. I used it for years when I was in charge of the Christmas programs at church. I'm sure the material will be suitable for your country school. Will you be in church on Sunday? If so, I'll give it to you before the service begins."

She sounded genuinely pleased to be able to help me yet again. I thanked her profusely and agreed to see her in church.

When I arrived at the church on Sunday morning, Hazel was waiting for me in the foyer. She handed me a bag containing the promised book and some other material that she thought I could use. With relief and gratitude I accepted it all and promised to return it in good condition.

"No, it is for you," she said. "I am no longer directing Christmas programs and you can use it."

"Thank you so much," is all I could say to that gracious, generous lady.

On Monday morning the children returned to school, anxious to tell me about their holiday experiences. Their excited chatter continued until I rang the bell for school to begin.

"It sounds like you all had a good Thanksgiving weekend, and we will soon be celebrating another holiday!" I said.

"Christmas!" they sang out in unison before I had asked the question.

"You're right!" I replied with enthusiasm, "and we will be doing a lot of exciting things this Christmas season: making Christmas cards and presents for our parents and decorations for our room. We have also been asked to put on a Christmas program for our families and friends. It is to be held in the evening, before our vacation begins. Of course, we have our regular lessons too; so it is going to be a very busy three weeks. Are we up to it?

An enthusiastic "Yes" was the answer and their positive response erased any lingering doubts in my mind. We would do our best and that would be good enough.

We adjusted our schedule to provide an hour a day to the program. The other Christmas projects would be dealt with as the schedule allowed and lessons were completed. The help of the older students was indispensible.

By the end of the first week we had a design for the Christmas program and had selected the performers for the Nativity scene. We decided that the main characters should be portrayed by the older children. Ruth Knox, an excellent reader, was chosen to be the narrator. Tom Teasdale was to be Joseph and Patsy Becker, Mary. Leo Dakin, Earl Manning, and Ron Teesdale agreed to be wise men. Julie Holden was chosen to be the angel. Jim Long, along with Donald and Jerry Manning, would be shepherds.

The younger children would recite poems (pieces) and sing "Away in a Manger". They would also join the older children in singing the carols interspersed throughout the program.

Two weeks before the program found the school a beehive of activity. While some children were occupied with their lessons; others were cutting, pasting, and coloring decorations and Christmas cards or working on gifts for their parents.

On Thursday afternoon we were presented with an additional challenge: Marvin Jewell stopped by with a beautiful tree that, when placed in the front corner of the room, almost reached to the ceiling. With all there was to do, decorating the tree became a priority. With some decorations donated by the parents and a few others from our local dime store, added to those made by the children, the tree looked beautiful!

By Friday afternoon the decorating was complete, the Christmas cards were ready to deliver to parents and friends, and the program had been rehearsed at least once. I praised the children for all they had accomplished in so short a time.

We returned to school on Monday, the week of the performance, to find a stage had been set up in the front of the room. As the children arrived I received the news that the Baptist minister's wife would stop by that morning to accompany them as they practiced the carols for the program. The event that had caused me so many sleepless nights was rapidly approaching!

The children came into the room and looked around in dazed silence. The stage, with the piano to its right, now occupied the front of the room. All the desks, mine included, had been moved back. A brief search was conducted before everyone was in the proper seat and the school day could begin.

The tension in the room was replaced by laughter as I stepped onto the stage to make announcements. "What a surprise to arrive this morning to find the room all set up for our program on Friday evening!" They nodded in agreement as I continued. "Later this morning the pianist will arrive. When she comes we will stop our work, welcome her, and listen carefully as she gives us directions. It is very nice of her to volunteer to do this for us, so be sure to thank her before she leaves."

At that point, we returned to our regular regimen. Once we found the flag, we recited the pledge of allegiance, followed by the singing of "America". Finally, to keep the story fresh, I read of the birth of Jesus from the book of "Luke".

The kindergarten reading class had just begun when there was a knock on the door. I opened it to find a tall, handsome woman, with a warm, friendly smile. "You must be the pianist," I said. "Please come in. I really appreciate your offer to play for us. I'm Beverly Haskins, the teacher."

"And I am Mrs. Huizinga," she said. "My husband is the pastor of the Baptist Church down the road."

I took her coat and hung it with mine behind the door; then turned and introduced her to the children. "Boys and girls, this is Mrs. Huizinga who is going to play the piano for us. Would you tell her good morning?"

That many of the children already knew and liked her was evident, as they greeted her by name.

I went to my desk and returned with a Manila folder which I handed to her, saying "This is a copy of the program with the songs and singers underlined. You can take some time to look it over if you wish, and we will begin the rehearsal whenever you are ready."

A brief glance at the material was all she required, and in a few minutes she was ready to begin. She encouraged the children to go to the middle of the stage, stand tall, sing so that the people in the back of the room could hear, and smile.

The children responded enthusiastically, and soon their voices accompanied by the piano filled the school with lovely music.

The rehearsal had ended and, as she was getting ready to leave, Mrs. Huizinga turned to me and asked when we might be practicing again.

"I plan to have a final rehearsal on Thursday morning at ten," I replied, "as the kindergarten children leave at eleven-thirty."

To my delight she offered to return on Thursday and remain for the entire production. "It's no trouble," she said, "I enjoy working with the children. By the way, can you use any costumes? We have some at the church that we won't be using this year."

I thought of the ill-fitting bathrobes and pieces of fabric we had intended to use, and gratefully accepted her offer.

On Thursday morning, Mrs. Huizinga returned, bearing her copy of the program and the promised costumes. With our help the actors found the appropriate garments and, with some reluctance, agreed to wear them. A smooth rehearsal followed, and by lunchtime all agreed that we were ready for the performance!

Friday, the day of the program, was a day of celebration. Our preparation was complete; it was time to relax and enjoy the season. I decided to spend the day reading stories, singing Christmas songs, sharing holiday plans, and playing games. Some children brought cookies to share, and I had a little gift for each child. Even the weather cooperated, for midway through the morning snow began to fall, gently, like a benediction.

It was nearly time for dismissal when someone knocked on the back door. I answered it, expecting to find a parent who had come early because of the snow and the evening program. Instead, to my astonishment, I came face to face with my fiancé, Louis Reyner. He was home on a Christmas furlough, and decided to surprise me, which he definitely did. I closed the door and gave him a warm welcome before inviting him inside to meet the children who seemed quite impressed with the tall, handsome, soldier in dress uniform, who was "Teacher's Boyfriend". He stayed a few minutes visiting with the children; then left for Grand Rapids where we would meet later.

Before long the parents arrived to take the children home where they could eat and prepare for the evening's program. I could guess at one topic of conversation around the dinner tables that night.

By six o'clock, when the children were told to be back at the school, the room was nearly full; by seven, when the program was to start, every seat was taken, and people were sitting on desktops and window sills. Some people were left standing, leaning against the walls.

Despite the crowd and my previous anxiety, I felt strangely calm and was able to pass the feeling to the children. Mrs. Huizinga, with her cheerful personality, encouraged them also, and they responded with a perfect performance.

The program was to end with everyone singing "Silent Night". Instead, to my surprise, the piano rang out and the crowd began to sing "Jingle Bells". Right on cue the back door opened and in came Santa Clause, carrying a big bag of goodies, which he promptly began distributing to the excited children.

As the crowd was beginning to disburse, Mr. Teesdale approached me with an invitation that made me aware that he knew of my company at home. "You can leave whenever you wish, Miss Haskins," he said. "The program was very good, but I'm sure you want to get home to enjoy the holidays. Don't worry about things here; the room will be in good order when you return. You just go on and have a Merry Christmas."

"Oh, I almost forgot," he said as, with a smile, he handed me a long white envelope. "Here is your paycheck and a little Christmas gift from all of us."

With that he went to join the others, while I gathered my belongings, wished a Merry Christmas to everyone, and left for Grand Rapids.

# CHAPTER 9

## Building Improvements

Suddenly the holiday season was over. The cards and decorations were stored away in the attic until their resurrection the following year. The Christmas tree, relegated to the backyard from its place of prominence in the living room, was becoming a shelter for birds and rodents. Louis had returned to his base, and the joyous holidays would soon become fond memories.

It was Monday morning and I was on my way back to school after a ten day vacation. Traffic was heavy and the tail lights from the cars ahead formed a red ribbon that penetrated the heavy fog associated with the January thaw in Michigan. The weak light from the lampposts revealed the fading holiday decorations that now looked sad and outdated.

As I turned north on Alpine Avenue, a grey dawn was breaking. The fog was lifting, but the landscape it revealed was devoid of color. I was driving through a grey world. Remembering the post-Christmas melancholy of my childhood, I spent the rest of my trip thinking of ways to create a cheerful classroom atmosphere on a dull, dreary, day.

I arrived at the school early, as planned; intending to put away the last remnants of the holidays before the children should arrive. Wading through slush, I made my way to the front door, unlocked it, and went inside. When I turned on the lights, I encountered a delightful surprise. The dull exterior gave way to a bright interior!

The room had been thoroughly cleaned and every vestige of Christmas cleared away. The floors had been polished until they shone. The chalkboard was green again, with no dulling chalk dust. But most amazing were two new doors on the back wall; one marked BOYS and the other GIRLS. We had INDOOR BATHROOMS! I removed my boots, hung my coat on the hook behind the door, and went to check out these wonderful additions to our classroom.

The girl's bathroom was bright and clean, with two stalls and shelves for supplies. The boy's room, approximately the same size and spotless, had only one stall and the strangest looking sink I had ever seen. It could accommodate several boys at a time. I couldn't conceive why that should be necessary, but never having been inside a boy's bathroom, I decided that this must be a normal appliance for male lavatories.

Now, however, there was work to be done, and the children would be arriving soon. My desk was piled high with school supplies, including those for the new bathrooms. I set to work sorting and distributing these to the proper shelves and cabinets. When the room was in order and the desktop finally cleared, I sat down to review my lesson plans and prepare for the arrival of the children.

I was writing the day's assignments on the chalkboard when the students began to arrive. Their cheerful greetings were music to my ears. There was no sign of post-holiday blues here; just the voices of children who were glad to be back at school with their friends.

They entered as a group all talking at once, describing their Christmas gifts and adventures. Suddenly they became aware of the changes in the room. "Wow, look at the floor. We could slide on it," said one. "Hey, the chalkboard is green," exclaimed another. But soon all attention was focused on the back of the room when someone shouted, "Look, inside toilets!"

"Put your coats and other belongings in the cloakroom," I instructed, "before you examine the new bathrooms. You still have ten minutes before school starts to catch up on all the news."

After their curiosity was satisfied, the children gathered in small groups to display their new acquisitions or tell of their holiday adventures. Several came to the desk where I was marking the attendance to ask what I had received for

Christmas and to check my finger for a ring. They were disappointed when I showed them the gift I had received from Louis, although they politely said that the watch was pretty.

At eight-thirty I rang the bell and school began in the usual way, with the pledge of allegiance to the flag and singing of "America". Then I invited any who wished to tell about one special gift they had received for Christmas. Several of the younger children eagerly responded, and we spent some time hearing about all of the wonderful presents that Santa had left under their trees.

Next it was time for announcements. I began by stating how appreciative I was of the nice, clean, classroom and especially the new bathrooms. I suggested that we all work together to keep our school clean and in good shape. Regarding the bathrooms, I set down a few simple rules.

No more than two were to be in the lavatory at any given time. They were to be sure to flush the toilets after using them. And finally, it was important to wash their hands afterward; the girls were to use the sink in the back of the room and the boys the new large sink on their bathroom wall.

The children were beginning their lessons when Ronnie Teesdale came to my desk where I was gathering up the kindergarten material for the first class of the day. "Teacher," he said, in a soft voice that was almost a whisper, "that isn't a sink in the boy's bathroom, it's a urinal."

"Oh," I said, in a voice that revealed my ignorance; then in a quieter voice, "thank you for telling me, Ron."

He returned to his seat, and immediately had his face, which was probably as red as mine, buried in his book. The other children appeared deeply engrossed in whatever they were studying, although I am sure they were fully aware of the conversation that had just taken place. The topic was never discussed in the classroom again, but before the day was over, all the boys and girls were using the sink in the back of the room. The older boys were wonderful mentors!

I thought my faux pas was buried until years later when I learned that it had been the topic of entertainment among the farmers who gathered at Fonger's General Store. My ignorance, it was decided, was due to my youth and sheltered environment. The students were educating their teacher!

The January thaw lasted for another week, by which time the playground had turned into a muddy lake. Indoor recess activities were becoming tiresome. We all were looking for a change in the weather, and on Friday afternoon it arrived. The clouds that had been absorbing moisture and hiding the sun for so long began to relinquish their heavy loads. The sky darkened and the rain began to fall just as the students were leaving for home. I hoped they had arrived there without getting too wet.

I made some plans for the week ahead, gathered my belongings, and was ready to leave, when the rain turned into a downpour. It showed no sign of letting up, so I turned off the lights, locked the door, and headed for my car. By that time I unlocked it and was inside my hair and coat were soaked! I turned around to see my umbrella lying on the back seat. "What we need is a big umbrella to leave in the entry for days like this," I decided. Another lesson was learned the hard way.

The sky was getting dark and the wind was picking up, so I decided to bypass the farm and head for Grand Rapids. I turned on my headlights, and my windshield wipers were making a swishing sound as they worked hard to clear away the torrent they confronted.

All at once the rain diminished and a new sound could be heard as hail hit the roof of the car and bounced off the windshield. Traffic slowed to a crawl, and the road became slick and dangerous. Finally I arrived home, late for dinner, damp, and tired, but glad to arrive safely.

All outside events were canceled for the evening and television reception was terrible, so the family sat around the dining room table playing cards. Mother made some popcorn, and later we had cake and coffee. The storm was forgotten as we enjoyed a rare evening together.

During the night a cold front arrived and by morning the ground was covered with a blanket of snow. We did the necessary shopping as early as possible because the weather forecast for the rest of the weekend was not encouraging. After a lunch of hot chicken soup I went to work preparing lesson plans, correcting papers, and grading report cards for the end of the semester.

Sunday morning dawned bright and clear, with an accumulation of six inches of fresh snow on the ground. The air was cold and crisp as we walked the mile to church, but the return trip proved less enjoyable. We were facing a cold wind from the west that made our eyes water and our noses turn red. By the time we arrived home I had decided to leave for the farm as soon as possible. The wind would be blowing across the roads I traveled and could soon make them impassable.

Mother had a delicious roast beef dinner waiting, and convinced me to eat before leaving. She argued that I would need something warm inside to sustain me should I encounter trouble on the road. I didn't want to consider that possibility, but decided to heed her wishes and sat down to a typical Sunday dinner with my family.

As soon as possible I excused myself, loaded my car, offered my farewells, and was on my way back to the farm. It was just in time, as the southbound lane was already filling with snow, and in places it was necessary to drive on the shoulder to allow oncoming traffic to pass. The country roads, sheltered by trees and buildings, were in better condition; so I cautiously continued on my way.

It was dark when I finally arrived at the farm. The Duforts were anxiously awaiting my arrival. They had called my home to find that I had left some time ago, and feared that I was stuck in a snow bank somewhere. Harry worked for the Kent County Road Commission during the winter and had already received calls for assistance. After they were assured that I was fine, we gathered in the living room to watch television and enjoy popcorn and apples.

When it was time for bed the wind was still howling around the house, but it did not disturb me. I felt safe and sound and, tired as I was, I fell asleep as soon as my head hit the pillow.

The next morning I awoke to the sun shining through my window. The sky was blue, and the fresh snow on the trees and the roofs of outbuildings glistened like diamonds. I dressed hurriedly and went downstairs to breakfast.

"What a beautiful day!" I said to Ellen as I entered the kitchen.

"Don't let it fool you," she replied. "It's five degrees out there. Harry and Bob have cleaned your windshield and swept the snow from your car, but they weren't able to get it started. They are pulling it around the driveway with the tractor now, trying to start the engine."

She put a hot breakfast of bacon and eggs on the table, and encouraged me to sit down and eat. Lorraine joined us shortly, and asked if the heater in her car had been turned on in preparation for her commute to her job in Grand Rapids. Evidently, although such service was a luxury to me, it was taken for granted here.

We were still at the table when Harry and Bob came in from outdoors. They stamped the snow from their boots before stepping into the kitchen.

"Your cars are ready, Ladies," said Harry, and looking at me continued, "We had to take your Ford for a little trip around the yard to get it started, but it's ready to go now. Drive carefully, both of you. The roads have been plowed, but there are some slippery spots."

I thanked both of them sincerely. I had never received such kindness, even from my own family. It was a service that I would receive many times before the long, cold winter was over.

# CHAPTER 10

## Visits and Invitations

January and February proved to be two of the coldest months on record. With the help of Harry and Bob I managed to get to school every day, but that was not the case with my students. Perfect attendance records were broken, as respiratory diseases spread through the school. I disregarded tardiness, as almost all of the children walked to school, some over a mile, often through blowing and drifting snow. Miraculously a majority of them, rosy cheeked and bundled to the chin, arrived on any given morning; so school was never cancelled.

Generally the children only missed a day or two of school, but Linda Dakins was not so fortunate. Her brother and sisters arrived one morning to report that she wouldn't be able to come back to school for at least a week because she had chicken pox.

For the next several days, whenever I met with the third grade class, I thought about Linda and what she was missing. The third grade is a transitional time in elementary education, when the child learns to read books without pictures, perform more complex math problems, and write proper sentences. Linda was doing a good job keeping up with her class but, as she was by nature shy, I was afraid that she would be discouraged if she fell behind.

After school as Leo and Donna were finishing the janitor work I made a decision. I had never known a teacher to make a house call and didn't know if I might be setting a precedent but decided that in this case it was necessary.

"Leo and Donna," I said, "I would like to stop by your house on my way home from school to help Linda catch up on the work she is missing. Would you ask your parents if that would be acceptable, and if so when I might come?" Their smiles said more than their words as they nodded their affirmatives.

The following morning the Dakins children arrived earlier than usual, and as soon as they had removed their wraps and deposited them in the cloakroom, all three came to my desk. As I expected, Leo was the spokesman.

"Miss Haskins," he said, "We told our mom and dad what you said, and Mom wonders if you could come tomorrow and stay for dinner."

The children were looking up at me with hopeful expressions on their faces as I paused a minute to consider any other commitments I might have made; but I quickly decided that nothing was more important than this invitation, so I responded enthusiastically. "Tell your mother I would be happy to come tomorrow, and I appreciate the invitation to dinner with your family."

The following day I was rewarded with a smile whenever one of the Dakins children caught my eye. At recess I took them aside to tell them that I was looking forward to the evening at their house and that they could ride there with me when the janitor work was done. With Lorene helping, Donna and Leo finished their work in no time; in fact, I was still correcting papers when they informed me that they were ready to go.

While I gathered my belongings and put on my coat and boots they went outdoors, without my asking, to clean the snow off my car and scrape the ice from the windshield. When I arrived and unlocked the car, I said a little prayer that my Ford would start. It had been sitting out doors in the cold school yard all day with the wind blowing around it and had demonstrated many times its preference for warm weather. We all hopped in and, when I turned the key in the ignition, the engine started without a hitch.

We arrived at the Dakins home in a matter of minutes and pulled in the driveway which had been recently cleared of snow. The children raced to the door and opened it to the delicious smell of roast beef and apple pie. I felt guilty in the knowledge that Mrs. Dakins had gone to such effort to accommodate "The Teacher."

The house was immaculate, and although not big, looked very comfortable. Leo took my wraps, while his mother welcomed me and led me into the living room where Linda was anxiously waiting.

The others left the room and I joined Linda on the sofa. At first, to put her at ease, we discussed the chicken pox, which I had also endured as a child. I told her how much we missed her at school, and how glad we were that she was getting better. She became more talkative as the minutes passed, and began asking about her classmates and the other children.

Finally we got around to her schoolwork. For nearly two hours we worked together, covering the lessons she was missing in social studies, math, English, and science. She read aloud from her literature book, and correctly answered my questions about the content. I was surprised and pleased to find that we had completed a day's work in so short a time. Finally I handed her the books and assignments for her to use as she felt able, along with some extra paper and pencils.

By now I noticed the other children appearing from wherever they had been hiding, and I knew that it must be time for dinner. Sure enough, Lorene popped into the room; "Mom says to tell you that dinner is ready," She announced.

The meal tasted as good as it smelled, and I enjoyed the fellowship of the family around the table; but it was already dark and the country roads were risky, so I soon thanked my hostess and prepared to leave.

Both parents and all the children thanked me sincerely for coming, and I left with the knowledge that I had done the right thing. Linda would perform as well as any in her class, and the family-school relationship was strengthened.

The days passed and the cold spell continued, but there was no need for additional home visits. As we adjusted to the weather, respiratory problems decreased and school attendance improved. We also developed a genuine appreciation for the new indoor bathrooms!

The children were tired of the confinements of the schoolroom and occasionally a few of the more adventurous would, at recess time, struggle into their heavy outerwear and spend a little time trying to construct a snowman or fort out of the intractable snow. When they found it impossible to form even a snowball they came back inside, defeated but energized.

Valentine's Day came, providing a welcome diversion from the winter doldrums. Early in the week I asked the children how they usually celebrated the event. They told of parties and decorations and of making and exchanging valentines; and, as they spoke, happy anticipation appeared on their faces.

I suggested that they spend the day getting some ideas for a party and talking them over with their friends at recess. Then, in the morning, we could decide how we wanted to celebrate. I reminded them that the kindergarten must be included in our plans.

Before leaving that afternoon I checked the art supplies to make sure there was a sufficient amount for twenty-five children to make valentines, and also decorations for the room. To be sure, I went home by way of the little village of Sparta and purchased all of the red construction paper and white doilies in the local dime store.

For the next day or two the children spent every spare minute creating, constructing, and composing valentines for their parents, grandparents, and anyone else they held dear. If I was busy teaching a class, the younger children asked the older ones for help, especially with spelling. Before long even the kindergarteners could write the whole sentence, "I Love You."

With the permission of the parents, the party was held in the afternoon. Some mothers came, with toddlers in tow, carrying plates of cookies or pitchers of punch. Everyone seemed to enjoy the games the children had chosen, but the highlight of the party was when the students received the valentines from one another. One student, a good reader, was chosen to open the decorated mailbox and deliver the envelopes to the hopeful recipients. The responses I observed when the mail was opened included smiles and laughter, and some shy blushes. I also received my valentines, and took them home to read and treasure.

At the end of the month a warming trend moved into the area, just in time for the President's Day holiday. The warm wind from the southwest joined with the occasional bursts of sunlight to melt the ice on the roads and soften the snow banks, providing construction material for snowballs, forts, and snowmen. By the time school was dismissed on Friday afternoon, the children were anxious to head for home to enjoy a long weekend of winter fun. I watched them as they walked down the road, stopping now and then to scoop up a handful of snow for a snowball which was aimed in the general direction of some target, usually a best friend. Their happy voices resounded in my ears, as I prepared to leave for my own three day vacation.

When I arrived at the farm to prepare for a weekend in Grand Rapids, Ellen greeted me with her usual friendly smile and handed me an envelope. "This came in the mail today," she said. "I thought you would want to see it before you left for the city."

I took the envelope and was surprised to see that it contained a letter from Mrs. Reyner, Louis's mother. She was inviting me to Petoskey for the Easter weekend. The family would be getting together, and my visit would provide an opportunity to meet his brothers and their families and become better acquainted with his parents.

I shared the letter with Ellen, and we agreed that I certainly should accept the invitation. Louis had told me about his brothers and shown me pictures of his nephews and niece, but we had never had an occasion to get to know one another. Now that the opportunity had arrived, I felt a little anxious about the prospect of confronting the whole family.

Ellen gave an encouraging laugh and told me that I had nothing to worry about. "Bev, when they get to know you, they will love you just like we do," she said. I thanked her for those kind words, although I wasn't sure I believed them. However, I gave her a hug before going to my room to pack for the trip home.

Though Easter was still over a month away, I had little time to prepare for such an important occasion. The weekends provided my only opportunity to shop and my wardrobe consisted almost entirely of the skirts and blouses I wore to school; nothing I felt suitable for an Easter encounter with my future in-laws.

My sister Betty and I shared a bedroom, and although she was several years my senior, we became close friends. She was my mentor and often in the evening before we went to sleep we had long talks, about anything from religion to men or even politics. That night we talked about meeting the families of our future husbands. She insisted that first impressions were very important, and with that she offered to go shopping with me to help me pick out the proper outfit for the occasion.

The downtown department stores didn't open until ten o'clock, so we enjoyed a leisurely breakfast with time to peruse the Easter ads in the Grand Rapids Press. As the weather in Petoskey was always colder than down state, we agreed that a suit would fit the occasion better than one of the fancy dresses pictured in the newspaper.

When it was time to leave we decided to take the bus instead of the car. The bus stop was only a block away, and a bus would take us right to the heart of town. In addition, we wouldn't have to deal with traffic and a parking meter.

The weather was warmer than it had been in weeks, so we didn't mind the short wait at the corner; and the ride provided time to discuss the styles and colors I preferred.

We spent the whole day looking for the suit I had in mind, taking time out for only a quick lunch at a little restaurant just off Monroe Street, one that Betty frequented when she worked downtown. We had covered the major department stores in the morning with no success. The suits that I liked were either the wrong size or the price was prohibitive. In the afternoon we visited the smaller ladies shops, where the latest styles on display appealed to neither my taste nor budget. We returned home after the shops closed, with nothing but white gloves to show for all our effort.

Shops were closed on Sunday in observance of the Sabbath, so I spent the day with family and friends. It was truly a day of rest.

Monday was President's Day and only stores that sold necessities like food or medicine were open. I spent the morning doing my laundry and browsing the Sears Roebuck Catalogue, considering the possibility of ordering a suit by mail. In the afternoon I headed back to the farm, arriving just in time for dinner.

As I joined the family around the table, I was greeted with the inevitable question, "How was your weekend?" I couldn't hide my disappointment as I described the fruitless shopping expedition. "I am even considering ordering a suit from the Sears Roebuck catalogue," I said, "but I don't know if I would receive it in time or if I would like it when I saw it; and what would I do if it didn't fit?"

As usual, Ellen provided a possible solution to my problem. "Della Holden, the mother of the Holden girls, is an accomplished seamstress. She has made clothing for people in this area and also in Grand Rapids, and she does excellent work. Maybe she would have time to make a suit for you before Easter."

"That's a wonderful suggestion," I replied enthusiastically. "I'll give her a call right after dinner."

When the meal was cleared away and the dishes done I made my call. One of the girls answered the phone, and was surprised when I asked for her mother. Soon Della Holden came to the phone. "Hello," she said in a friendly voice.

I stated my request, and her response was just what I hoped. "Let's get together later this week. You can look through my pattern book and pick out a suit you like."

Early the following morning, Julie Holden came to my desk and gave me a sweet smile as she said, "Mom says Thursday would be a good time for you to come over and look at some patterns; she would like you to stay to dinner too."

"Thank your mother for the invitation and tell her that Thursday would be just fine with me, and I am looking forward to spending some time with your family," I responded.

Two days later I spent a very productive and enjoyable afternoon and evening at the Holden home. Della and I browsed through the pattern book until I found the suit I liked; then she measured me to determine how much material and other supplies I should purchase. Finally she drew up a list that included this information and places to shop for the best quality and price.

While we were busy inside, the girls were outdoors helping their father with the chores. When they came in, I was impressed by the way they worked together to help their mother put the meal on the table, one that she had prepared earlier in the day. It was delicious and hot from the oven.

As we sat around the table I noted the harmony within the family. The girls, although completely different in appearance and personality, seemed to enjoy being together; and all three showed love and respect for their parents. I thoroughly enjoyed the meal and conversation, and was sorry when it was time to leave.

I thanked Della for the wonderful evening and her delicious meal, and promised to return with the material for the suit as soon as possible.

"That's good," she responded. "Easter is only five weeks away, and I have a lot of projects to complete by then."

# CHAPTER 11

## Spring At last

March came in like a lion. After the late February thaw that melted most of the snow, winter returned with a vengeance. We were greeted with a cold wind from the north, accompanied by an occasional blast of flurries.

Back at the schoolhouse the children were disappointed with the weather. It was too cold and windy for outdoor activities, and the snowflakes did not elicit the happy response they had in November. The kindergarteners were dubious when we compared the pictures on the calendar with what they observed through the window. I tried to console them with the promise that spring was just around the corner; soon they too would be running around outdoors, playing ball, flying kites, and enjoying the playground equipment.

We talked about the signs of spring. "Let's be on the lookout for buds on the trees or flowers peeping up through the ground. I wonder who can see the first robin." I said.

Their spirits lifted a bit as they followed my instructions to draw pictures of signs of spring. I promised to place their work on the bulletin board and, if they found anything outdoors that was in their pictures, they could mark it with a gold star.

The month of March brought concerns more important than the weather. It was time to measure the progress the children had made academically under my instruction. The annual achievement tests were to be administered and sent to the county board of education before the end of the month.

The very thought of taking a standardized test is daunting for some children, so I spent time providing individual instruction for those who might have trouble with the testing process. In addition, each grade was led through a quick review of the subject matter that had been covered since school began in September. When it was time to administer the tests I felt that my students were well prepared.

In addition to passing the achievement tests, the eighth graders were required to be able to recite THE GETTYSBURG ADDRESS and THE PREAMBLE TO THE CONSTITUTION before they graduated in June. They practiced whenever they had free time and, as they repeated the words, I observed the younger children saying them right along with them. I wondered how much the little ones had already learned by just listening and observing.

When the busy week was over, I headed back to Grand Rapids to take care of personal concerns. The first item on my agenda was another shopping trip. Betty had other plans and did not accompany me this time but, thanks to Della Holden, I knew just where to shop and what to buy. I found what I was looking for in just over an hour, and was amazed at how much less the materials for the suit cost than a finished garment of like quality. After paying Mrs. Holden her asking price, and perhaps a little more, I would still save a considerable amount. Encouraged by my good fortune, I rewarded myself with a counter lunch at the downtown FIVE and DIME before catching a bus back home.

My mother, although not a professional seamstress, had made most of the clothing for my sisters and me when we were growing up. She had never, however, attempted anything as challenging as my suit. Although no longer physically able to take on such a project, I am sure she would have enjoyed trying. She studied the pattern carefully and stroked the material, before handing it back to me with a sigh. "It should look very nice on you," she said.

After school was dismissed on Monday afternoon I stopped at the Holden house and presented Della with the results of my shopping expedition. She emptied the bags and, after looking over the contents, said with a smile, "It looks like we have everything we need. I'll be starting on your suit as soon as possible. I'm working on Easter outfits for my girls too, but I'm sure I can have you all looking beautiful for the holiday."

At dinner, back at the farm, I thanked Ellen again for suggesting that I contact Mrs. Holden. "Just make sure we get to see you in that outfit before you head for Petoskey," was her reply.

On Wednesday morning I arrived at school to discover a package on my desk. I opened it to find the achievement tests and directions for administering them. I had time to give the material only a quick perusal before the children began arriving, but decided to study it thoroughly at home that evening. This would be my first experience in giving a standardized test, and I felt a little nervous about procedure.

After dinner, instead of joining the Dufort family for a pleasant evening of television, I went directly to my room to review the directions for administering the exam and make sure that the package included the proper number of booklets for students in grades four through eight. According to the instructions, the tests should be given when the room was quiet and the students were relaxed. That would be in the afternoon, after the kindergarten had been dismissed.

In the morning I announced that the tests had arrived and that grades four through eight would begin testing after the noon recess. I suggested that they go outdoors for some fresh air and exercise after eating, and use the restrooms and drinking fountain when they came in, as they would need to remain in their seats while taking the tests.

I turned to the younger children and said, "The room must be absolutely quiet while the older children are testing. That means the rest of you, except for the kindergarteners who will go home at their usual time, must remain in your seats also. Your math assignment will be on the board; after you finish, you may work on an art project or read one of the books from the shelves in the back of the room. Please gather everything you will need before lunchtime."

Addressing the whole class, I asked, "Are there any questions?"

When no one responded I realized that the students were already familiar with the testing process; the only one new to the game was the teacher!

Although the weather was chilly, the bright sun gave the illusion of warmth and everyone willingly went outdoors for a short recess. When I rang the bell they came in quietly, and after hanging up their wraps and stopping at the water faucet and the rest rooms, quietly took their seats and waited patiently for the ordeal to begin.

I presented each child with a test booklet, which was not to be opened until I gave the signal to start, and a sharpened No. 2 pencil. When everyone was ready, I said "Go", and suddenly the only sound to be heard was the ticking of the clock.

After an hour and a half of silence, my voice sounded unusually loud as I said, "Close your booklets and lay down your pencils. You did an excellent job, and now you deserve an extra long recess. Get up and move about and go outdoors if you wish."

As I packaged the completed tests for mailing to the county board of education, I heaved a sigh of relief knowing that the process wouldn't be repeated until the following year.

Spring was slow to arrive that March. The snow flurries turned to cold rain, followed by an occasional sunny day. Turbulent weather, including a tornado, struck the east side of the state, while we experienced only a thunderstorm. Despite the weather, the younger children were able to find signs of spring.

Allen Norman and Steven Powell were first to claim success. "We saw a robin out by the barn!" they announced excitedly. Then they went on to tell everyone how they had recognized it. "It had a red chest, and a brown back," said Allen; while Steven nodded his head in agreement. As I had promised, I awarded each boy with a gold star, which he attached to his picture on the bulletin board.

The next day little Diana Davison came in with a bouquet of Pussy Willows. "My mother and I found these down by the marsh," she said.

Ruth Knox located a Mason jar in the storage room and helped Diana fill it with water before adding the delicate branches. After adding Pussy Willows to her picture of spring and affixing a gold star, Diana proudly mounted her picture with the others.

Wayne Wainwright brought in a Forsythia branch that was about ready to bloom. We could find only one Mason jar, so he added his treasure to Diana's Pussy Willows, creating an attractive bouquet which we enjoyed for weeks, as little green leaves developed adding to the color.

When Wayne had finished his picture, complete with his gold star, I thought the activity was finished; but I was wrong. By now some of the older children had joined in the game, and soon the bulletin board was covered with spring pictures, each adorned with at least one gold star.

The following week I received word from the Holden girls that my suit was ready, except for the hem. "Mom wants you to come over to try it on," said Carole.

"And stay for dinner," Ruth added shyly.

The next day I made the now familiar trip to the Holden farm. When I arrived the girls were doing their usual chores, so Della and I had privacy as I tried on the suit. While she measured and pinned up the hem, I learned a little about their family history.

Mr. Holden, Merlin, was from pioneer stock and had strong ties to the Gougeburg School. The land on which the school was located belonged to his parents, Lynn and Lola Holden, who offered the district a one hundred year lease with the provision that, should the land no longer be used as a school, it would revert to the family. Merlyn farmed the land around the school, as well as managing his own large dairy farm. He and Della had no sons, so their daughters became "farm girls" and, according to Carole, learned how to cook after they married.

Merlin Holden attended the Gougeburg School, as did his mother, Lola Davis Holden, whose parents, Matt and Maggie Davis, owned the farm at that time. When he was eight years old Merlin had polio, and the teacher walked to their house after school to help him with his lessons.

There is record of Matt's father, Alanson Davis, living in the Algoma area as early as the eighteen sixties; so Julie, Carole, and Ruth had a heritage that would provide the stability few children enjoy.

Della had just finished pinning my skirt and my history lesson ended, when Merlin and the girls came in from the barn. While they cleaned up and got ready for dinner, I helped Della in the kitchen. As we were eating, I looked at the family with new respect. Realizing how much they had already contributed to their community. I wondered what the girls would do with their legacy.

As I drove home it started to rain, and by the time I arrived back to the farm I saw a flash of lightening followed by a roar of thunder. I made a dash for the kitchen door, arriving just in time to avoid a downpour as the rain increased in intensity.

Ellen met me at the door as I came in carrying my shoes. "You must be soaked, child," she said, "Come on in and get warm."

"I'm just fine," I replied. "I just got a little damp coming from the car to the house and stepping in a puddle on the way."

"We were worried about you," said Harry from his chair in the living room. "Did you have any trouble on the road?"

"Not at all," I replied. "I'm sorry if I worried you. Mrs. Holden was telling about the family history while she fixed the hem in my suit, and by the time we had dinner it was already dark."

"Why don't you go upstairs and change into some dry clothes," Ellen said; "and by the way here is a letter for you that arrived this afternoon. I'm sure you will want to read it." With a knowing smile, she handed me the letter and I told them all goodnight and headed for my room.

After changing into my pajamas and hanging up my damp coat, I sat on the side of the bed and read a long letter from Louis.

My Dearest Beverly,

I can hardly wait for your visit next weekend. It seems so long since we've been together.

I have some good news for you: We have all been worried about your making the long trip to Petoskey from Grand Rapids alone, especially since your little car isn't always reliable; so I have decided to travel with you. My brother, Freal, has very generously offered the use of his car.

I plan to leave Petoskey on Thursday morning and pick up my transcripts from Calvin and Grand Rapids Junior College in the afternoon. Harold Hamilton has agreed to provide me with a letter of recommendation for the pre-ministry program at North Central College, and invited me to spend the night with them. I will meet you at the farm when you return from school on Friday; then we can be on our way north.

How does this sound to you? If there is a problem, please call me as soon as possible.

With all my love,

Louis

I put the letter aside and crawled under the covers. All night long wind blew and the rain pelted the house but, safe and secure in this home that had safely weathered many storms, I slept peacefully with pleasant dreams of the week ahead.

I woke in the morning with the sun shining brightly through my bedroom window and the smell of breakfast wafting up from the kitchen below. Invigorated by a sound sleep and feeling of spring in the air, I went downstairs humming the song from the play, OKLAHOMA, "Oh What a Beautiful Morning".

Ellen was in a cheerful mood too, as she greeted me with a smile. "That was quite a storm we had last night," she said. "I hope it didn't keep you awake."

"Not at all, I slept like a baby; and look at this beautiful sunshine! The kids will be chafing at the bit to get outdoors. I hope the ground dries up a bit before morning recess, or the younger children will be covered with mud.

They have spent so many recesses pent up inside that I haven't the heart to make them stay indoors on a beautiful day like this."

I told her about the letter from Louis, and she was pleased that he would be coming to make the trip north with me. "That's good. Harry and I didn't like the idea of you driving so far alone," she said.

Just then Lorraine came into the kitchen and joined us for breakfast. "What a storm," she said. "That thunder kept me awake all night. I don't know how I'll get through the day of work."

"Well it's certainly beautiful out there this morning," Ellen countered, and in good time too, just in time for Holy Week." Turning to me she added, "one week from today Beverly will be heading up to Petoskey for a very important event."

We shared our plans for the weekend as we finished our meal and prepared to go our separate ways: to work, to school, and to the grocery store. We wouldn't be together again until Monday evening.

The following week went by quickly. The month of March left like the proverbial lamb, and April ushered in the sunshine and blue skies that the children had been waiting for. Each recess found the playground equipment in use by the younger children, while the older ones enjoyed a perennial game of softball.

One day, when the kindergarten students were too distracted to keep their minds on the lesson, I sent them outdoors for an early recess. The little boys decided to try their hand at softball. The classroom was quiet and the older children were busy with their lessons, when the voice of Allen Norman came clearly through the open windows. "That's not the way you do it, Steve," he shouted. "I am supposed to hold the bat like this, see, and you hit the bat with the ball."

The room erupted with laughter and, as it was nearly recess time for all, I dismissed the rest of the children to enjoy some time in the sun. When they came in they were ready to resume their studies.

Easter was the theme of the art projects for the week, and I was surprised at the variety of ways the children depicted what the holiday meant to them. Some were willing to tell about their pictures, while other art needed no explanation. I taught them how to make simple baskets, and asked them each to produce a sturdy one by Friday morning.

On Wednesday, the Holden girls informed me that my suit was ready. I stopped to pick it up on my way home. Della insisted that I try it on one last time. It fit perfectly, and I was delighted with the quality of her work. I tried to pay her more than her asking price, but she would have none of it. She certainly had earned more than I paid.

She showed me the beautiful Easter dresses she had made for her girls, and I could envision them looking like little angels when they wore them to church on Sunday.

Friday morning arrived before we knew it. The children were excited with the coming holiday. Some were traveling, others having visitors, but everyone, it seemed, was planning a visit from the Easter Bunny.

All of the children were excused with the kindergarteners at eleven-thirty that day, but before they left I filled their baskets with jelly beans and a chocolate egg. I wished them a happy Easter and a great vacation, and told them that I would see them again in ten days.

A quick cleanup was all that was required to make the classroom look respectable, and I worked with Leo and Donna to finish the task in short order. Then I paid them their wages for the month and sent them happily on their way.

Finally, after locking the doors of the schoolhouse, I got in my car and headed for the farm. My excitement mounted as I realized that the adventure I had anticipated for so long was about to begin.

# CHAPTER 12

## Easter Vacation

I arrived at the farm to find Louis in the kitchen with the Dufort family. Because it was Good Friday Lorraine had the day off, and the men had evidently come in from the fields for lunch. "We've just been having a good talk with your young man here," said Harry, "kind of giving him a cross examination."

"Nothing of the sort," countered Ellen. "We've just been getting acquainted. We are about ready to sit down for lunch; do you have time to join us for a sandwich and cake before you head north?"

"If it is okay with Bev," Louis replied, "I would like to get started. We have a long way to go, and I'd like to get to Petoskey before dark. There is a little restaurant in Cadillac where we can stop for lunch. It's a good place for a break, and the food is excellent."

"That's fine with me," I responded. "I'll just go upstairs and change into something comfortable for the trip."

In a few minutes I returned, dressed in jeans and a sweater. I was carrying my small suitcase and had my Easter suit on my arm. "Can we just put these on the back seat?" I asked, "I don't want my suit to wrinkle."

"Sure, no problem," he responded "We have plenty of room. You had better take your coat though. It is pretty cold in Petoskey at this time of year, especially at night."

We had wished everyone a happy Easter and were going out the door when Ellen stopped me. She gave me a big hug and handed me a bag. "Here are some cookies to eat on your way," she said. "You may be hungry before you get to Cadillac."

It was shortly after noon when we left the farm. We were glad for the time to be alone together. We hadn't seen each other in several weeks, and there were things that couldn't be discussed on the telephone, especially on a party line. After filling each other in on what had been happening in our lives, we turned to talk of the future.

Louis began by reminding me of a letter he had sent from Japan telling me that he had felt a call to the ministry. Since his discharge and return to Petoskey, the invitation had become more frequent and persistent. After praying about it, he sought advice from Christians he knew and respected, including his pastor, John Murbach, who advised him to enroll in our denominational college, North Central, located in Naperville, Illinois.

I didn't take that news very calmly. I reminded him that we had spent most of our courtship separated by hundreds and even thousands of miles. "Why can't you just go back to Calvin and change your major from science to theology" I asked.

"Calvin would be ideal as far as location is concerned," he replied; "but I have problems with the Calvinist theology. I want to serve as a pastor in the Evangelical United Brethren Church and North Central is our nearest denominational college."

I was quiet, working on an attitude adjustment, when we came to the well known Cadillac Hill, dangerous for icy conditions or bad brakes. We didn't have to worry about either on this trip. We were over the rise and coming down the other side, when Louis pointed to his left and said, "There's the restaurant."

I turned to see a small, brick building with two large plate glass windows overlooking the highway. In front was a sign advertising "Johnie's Restaurant." We turned into a driveway that led to a parking lot at the back of the restaurant. It was full of cars, even though the time was well past the usual lunch hour.

We entered through the back door, and waited for several minutes for a waitress to locate and prepare an empty booth. She finally seated us in a corner away from the crowd. I looked around and wondered what brought people to this place; it certainly wasn't the ambience.

I ordered a sandwich and small salad, which provided my answer; the food was delicious. The house dressing was the best I had ever tasted, and the bread was straight from the oven. Louis had ordered a hamburger, which he was eating with relish. "Now you see why I chose this place," he said.

As we were finishing our meal we returned to the conversation we were having in the car. Louis began by saying, "I don't want another separation either, Honey, but it will only be for nine months, and I won't be so far away this time. Naperville isn't much farther than Petoskey, and there are four lane highways most of the way. Also, some seminary students come to Michigan every weekend to serve small rural churches. I could probably share the ride with one of them and you could pick me up at his destination. Anyway let's deal with that problem when we come to it. For now what do you say we turn to happier subjects? We have a great weekend ahead of us."

We finished our meal with small talk, and left the restaurant, satisfied by the food as well as our conversation.

As we continued, north our talk turned to plans for our wedding. We agreed that the ceremony should be in my church, as was customary. It was also the place where we first met and had spent significant time together.

We were in the process of choosing our wedding party when the car began to make an ominous sound. Louis checked the gas supply and reported no problem there. He pulled to the side of the road and checked the tires. They were in good shape. He was no mechanic, but he looked under the hood anyway. He got back in the car and reported, "I can't see anything wrong. Kalkaska is right ahead; we will have to stop there and find a mechanic."

We limped into town with the car making a noise that attracted the pedestrians who were enjoying a stroll among the quaint shops on Main Street. Louis stopped in front of the village park and suggested that I wait in the car while he tried to locate a mechanic who could come to our aid.

A young man, dressed in jeans and flannel shirt was coming out of the hardware store when Louie approached him and asked where he might find help. He pointed down the street and said, "There is a mechanic just around the corner. I think he closes at five o'clock, so you'll have to hurry if you want to catch him."

Louis headed for the corner and returned in a few minutes, followed by a middle aged man dressed in blue coveralls with the name "Chuck" embroidered on the pocket. He was carrying a flashlight and a wrench. "I only have a few minutes," he said as he lifted the hood and, with his flashlight, scanned everything underneath. "Get inside and start the engine," he said to Louis.

When Louis turned the key the engine turned over with a loud whine and a cough.

"I'm sorry to have to tell you this, young man," Chuck said, "but you have a serious problem with that engine; maybe valves, maybe a rod. I can't tell until I can get it into the shop. Like I said, it is past closing time, and my wife is unhappy when I'm late for dinner. It's Easter weekend too, so I won't be back to work until Monday. If you can bring it in then, I'll see what I can do for you."

"Thanks Chuck," Louie replied, "but we're on our way to Petoskey and we hope to get there tonight. I guess I will have to call my folks and see what can be arranged. By the way, is there a public phone nearby?"

"In the lobby of the hotel," Chuck replied, "just inside the door." He wished us good luck and hurried back to lock up his shop and head for home and dinner.

We stood on the sidewalk for a while, contemplating the situation. A big banner was over the street announcing the Trout Festival, which was to take place the following week. Placards in the store windows listed the entertainment and contests. It was probably the most exciting event of the year in the little town of Kalkaska, but we didn't feel very excited.

We walked around town considering our options, and wondering if there was anything we could have done to prevent the situation. Had we stopped at a garage in Cadillac could we have prevented the trouble? But why should we stop when we could detect no problem? We asked ourselves a dozen questions, before Louis finally said, "Dad should be home from work by now. I guess we should go into the hotel and give him a call."

The hotel lobby was tastefully decorated and large enough to accommodate a dozen people comfortably. An attractive receptionist was at the desk. She gave us a friendly smile. "Can I help you?" she inquired.

Louis told her the nature of our problem and she directed him to a small telephone booth next to her desk. It was almost hidden by a large plant and provided complete privacy to anyone making a call.

I found a comfortable seat nearby and while I waited the receptionist told me the proud history of the building. The hotel which was over a hundred years old had been in business, with few exceptions, since its construction. She offered to provide a tour, but Louis had just left the phone booth and was heading our way. A warm smile had replaced the worried look with which he had entered the hotel.

"Dad says not to worry," he said. "He and Mom are just having dinner and will head down here with the truck as soon as they finish and can get on the road. He doesn't drive very fast, so he suggested that we have something to eat while we wait for them to arrive."

As if on cue, the dining door opened and a delicious aroma wafted through the lobby. The receptionist, noting our hesitancy, said, "Why don't you stay and have dinner here while you wait? We have an excellent chef, and there is no better restaurant in the area."

The atmosphere in the dining room was warm and friendly and the food was good, so we lingered over our meal while we waited for his parents to arrive.

We were leaving the hotel and heading for the car when a truck came around the corner and, spotting us, pulled to the curb. Mr. and Mrs. Reyner came over to give us a warm welcome. They expressed their sincere concern about our car trouble. We assured them that everything had worked out all right; we made it into town without an accident and received some good advice from kind people.

Mr. Reyner didn't bother to look under the hood. Instead he turned to Louis and said, "How about giving me a hand with the chain? We can get hooked up and head for home in no time. As it is, it will be pretty late by the time we get there."

When the vehicles were attached securely, and otherwise prepared for the trip, we were on our way. His parents rode in the truck, while Louis and I were behind in the car. We rode with lights on, and I hoped that the battery was in good repair. We traveled a county road parallel to the highway, and encountered little traffic.

Once underway, we relaxed and enjoyed the trip. The weather was unseasonably warm, the sky was filled with stars, and the tree frogs were serenading us with their mating song. Louis kept his eye on the truck ahead, but gone was the anxiety of the afternoon. We talked about simple things or not at all, riding in silence, my head on his shoulder.

It was nearly midnight when we arrived in Petoskey. Mr. Reyner drove up the long hill leading to the Reyner home and parked the truck and car on the gravel road beside the house. We took our few belongings inside and headed for the bedrooms that Mrs. Reyner had prepared for us. I was assigned Louis' room upstairs in the front of the house, while he had his brother's room in the back. In no time at all we were all asleep and the house was quiet.

I woke the next morning to find everyone else had already begun their day. Louis had called his brother to tell him about our mishap, the car had been towed to the repair shop, and Mr. Reyner had gone on to work. Breakfast was waiting on the table.

I apologized for sleeping so late, but Louis excused me, saying, "We knew you were exhausted. After teaching all morning, the long trip, and the trouble on the road, you needed a good long rest. I hope you feel better this morning."

"Daddy had breakfast before he left for work, but Louis wanted to wait for you. I have had a cup of coffee earlier, but am a bit hungry now. Do you mind if join you?" Mrs. Reyner asked.

"I would be delighted!" I replied and Louis nodded in agreement. "It will give us a chance to become better acquainted."

While we ate Mrs. Reyner told us about the family:

She was born in Indiana, but had moved to Alanson, Michigan as a young girl. It was there she had met Mr. Reyner, who had come to work in his uncle's dairy. They were married in the Methodist Church in Alanson. They had four sons: Charles Marvin, who went by his second name, Freal, Lynn, who was in the air force and serving in England, and Louis, the youngest. She went on to tell of a sister, step-sister, and other more distant relatives.

After an hour or two, I could tell that Louis had his fill of family history, at least for the time being. He got up from the table and began clearing away the dishes and filling the sink with hot water. I excused myself, and joined him in the task, but not before I thanked my prospective mother-in-law for the information she had shared.

When the table was cleared and the dishes put away, Louis turned to his mother, who had retired to her rocker near the window. "Mom," he said, "I would like Bev to walk downtown with me and enjoy a tour of beautiful Petoskey. If she agrees, we won't be back for lunch."

He gave me a questioning smile, and I replied, "It sounds like a great idea."

I felt somewhat concerned about leaving Mrs. Reyner alone, but Louis assured me that she would be just fine. It was her habit to spend the morning in her rocker, napping most of the time.

I discovered that a walk in Petoskey was either uphill or down. We began by going down Howard Hill, until we came to the intersection with Mitchell Street. Along the way Louis pointed out his elementary school and the high school where he had enjoyed participating in basketball and band.

We spent some time exploring the businesses along Mitchell Street, everything from the library at one end to a gift shop at the other. The shop was owned and managed by a Chinese family, and contained merchandise from all over the world. We lingered there, admiring the unusual assortment of gifts and furnishings. I finally purchased a few items to share with my students when school resumed.

All the activity and exercise were making us hungry, so we decided to interrupt our exploration with lunch. "There is a little Greek restaurant called the Arcadia just up the street near the bank," Louis said. "The food is good, and I think you'll enjoy the atmosphere."

We headed back up the hill, but didn't go far before we came to what appeared at first glance to be a candy store, due to a large assortment of sweets in the front window. Upon entering, however, I was impressed by a very attractive dining room. Tall booths lined the outer walls; each with a jukebox where, for a nickel, patrons could hear their favorite song. Little table lamps provided the only illumination and added to the cozy atmosphere.

We ordered sandwiches and sodas, and Louis told me about growing up in this beautiful town on the bay. It seemed to me the perfect place to settle and raise a family. The schools were well rated, as were the hospitals and libraries.

There were plenty of activities for everyone, from children to senior citizens. In addition, the Bay View community just north of town offered a summer program of music and culture that was second to none.

"I agree with you, Honey, and I love this town, but don't get your heart set on living here. In our church, ministers are almost never assigned to preach in their home towns." Seeing my disappointment, he added, "Of course we can always come back on our vacations."

We turned back to talk of his family. I had noticed that his mother called him "Louis", while his father and the people we had met in town all called him "Louie."

"As my mother said, I was named after her. Her middle name is Lois, and Louis is as close as she could get in a boy's name. I think she really wanted a girl. For as long as I can remember everyone else has called me "Louie", and that's the name I'm most comfortable with, except for formal occasions; but you can call me whatever you wish, "Honey" or "Sweetheart" would do for starters.

"I think I'll stick with "Louie", I said, "except under certain circumstances," I added with a laugh.

We played one of our favorite songs, "In the Mood" by Glenn Miller, before leaving to resume our tour of the town.

Continuing down Howard Street to Lake Street we passed exclusive shops, the owners of which had not returned from Florida where they had other stores in the winter resorts. One business, an old fashioned general store, was open, and we looked around before purchasing a pound of gourmet coffee for Mr. and Mrs. Reyner.

From a bench in the city park on east Lake Street we could see the portico of the old Perry Hotel. It reminded me of pictures I had seen of anti-bellum buildings in the east.

"The building is not as old as it looks," Louie explained. "The original hotel was a much smaller building with big, white pillars in the front. After it burned to the ground, the new owners of the property, the Perry family, decided to build a hotel with architecture similar to the old train station on the other side of the street. The interior is decorated and furnished in vintage style. You should see it!"

"Do you suppose they would let us just go inside and see the lobby now", I asked. "I just love old buildings that are well preserved."

"It's early yet," he replied. "I don't think anyone would object."

We went inside and were admiring the lobby with its beautiful chandelier and sumptuous furnishings when we were approached by an attractive young lady who appeared to represent the management. We informed her that I was a visitor to Petoskey and, having heard of the hotel, had come inside to look around.

"Well, if you have time," she said with a pleasant smile, "I would love to give you a quick tour of the building."

We left the lobby and followed her up an open stairway to the second floor. I remarked about the carpeting which was almost a replica of that in my grandmother's big house on Sweet Street in Grand Rapids.

"You wouldn't believe the time we had locating that pattern. It was very popular at the turn of the century, but we had to go to Chicago to find anything even resembling the original." She said.

She opened a door on her left and we entered a room with windows that overlooked Little Traverse Bay. Louie pointed out the breakwater and the dock that would be crowded with boats after Memorial Day. The ball field where he played softball with the city team was near the waterfront. Harbor Springs was visible across the bay.

"Rooms with a view of the bay are preferred by most of our guests," our guide informed us. "However the rooms across the hall offer a lovely vista also."

She ushered us into a room opposite the one we had just visited. They were similarly decorated and furnished, but when she opened the drapes, we had a view of the picturesque little train station across the street and the city tennis courts just beyond.

"Both rooms are beautiful," I said. "Thank you for showing them to us. Either one would be a wonderful place to spend a night."

"We hope you will do just that, soon," she said.

Louis looked at his watch and said, "We really should be on our way. We have one more stop before we head to my folk's for dinner."

We walked back to Lake Street and went downhill until we came to a picturesque little park where the Bear River flowed over a little waterfall and made its way into the bay.

"This is called Mineral Well Park," Louie said. "Just take a drink from the fountain over there, and you'll know why." He pointed to a concrete structure not far away.

I did as he suggested; the smell of sulfur and the taste of a variety of minerals made me grimace; "It's horrible!" I said in disgust.

"Some people think it has curative powers," Louie replied, laughing. "They come from miles around to fill containers that they take home with them. Some take jugs full to Florida when they leave for the winter."

"It's time to head for home now, though. We have a few miles to walk, and it's uphill all the way."

Emmett Street was not as steep as Howard, but I could feel the muscles in my legs tighten as we resumed our walk. We crossed Mitchell Street by the Post office and were coming to a mostly residential area, when Louie stopped to point out the church we would be attending the next morning. It was a pretty, brick structure, on a little side street just off Emmett. We paused to check the sign in front that listed the time of the Easter services in the morning.

When we resumed our walk, my energy was waning, and I wondered whether I could make it up the Sheridan Street Hill. Just then a horn sounded and a truck pulled over. It was Louie's father on his way home from the Bremeyer-Bain

Hardware Store, where he worked as a plumber, electrician, and all-around skilled tradesman. Needless to say, we were happy to see him, and relieved when he offered us a ride the rest of the way home.

Mrs. Reyner was putting dinner on the table as we arrived. We shared our adventures of the day as we enjoyed her casserole and home baked biscuits, with chocolate pudding for dessert.

"You must be worn out with all that walking," she said. "You probably just want to relax tonight. Perhaps you would like to join us in playing some table game."

That was agreeable to everyone, and we enjoyed a friendly game of dominoes until Mr. Reyner reminded us that the next day was Easter Sunday and we might want to get up early for the Sunrise Service at church.

"If you would like to shower before you retire, Beverly," Mrs. Reyner said, "You will find everything you need on the little table in the bathroom." I thanked her for the invitation, and found the warm water just what I needed to relax my tired muscles.

Alone in the hallway, Louie and I were able to share a goodnight kiss before I headed for bed. I fell asleep almost immediately, and didn't remember a thing until the sun, which was just coming up over the horizon, awakened me in the morning.

I dressed carefully, enjoying the feel of my new clothes against my skin. After putting on my suit and adjusting the finishing touches, I admired my reflection in the big mirror which was over the chest of drawers. Taking my hat and purse from a little table nearby, I headed for the stairs hoping to make a positive impression on the most important family members.

Louie was in the shower, but Mr. Reyner was at the kitchen table preparing his Sunday school lesson for an adult class he was teaching. He looked up from his work. "Good Morning. You look very nice." He said, "Did you sleep well?"

"Very Well," I replied. "I think this northern air agrees with me."

Just then Louie stepped out of the bathroom, looking very handsome in grey trousers, a soft yellow shirt, and navy jacket. His tie was blue with grey stripes. His dark hair, still wet from the shower, was neatly combed in the style of the day.

He looked me over head to toe, and gave a low whistle. "You look great!" he said. "You'll be the prettiest girl in the church; won't she Dad."

Poor Mr. Reyner, not knowing how to respond, finally said, "She looks very nice."

I was beginning to feel embarrassed by all the attention, and was glad when Louie changed the subject to the plan for the morning. "Bev and I stopped by the church yesterday and noticed that there is a sunrise service at seven this morning, followed by a breakfast at eight. Are you and Mom going?" He asked his dad.

"No," he replied. "Your mother wants to get dinner in the oven. Freal, Mary, and the children will be joining us after church, and then we are all invited over to Harbor Springs for supper with Marvin and Kathryn. That will be all she can handle. However, if you and Beverly are going to the sunrise service you had better take the car. You don't want to be late," he said, as he handed Louie the keys.

We arrived at the church as the service was about to begin. The organ was playing softly and the congregation was seated, quietly listening to a medley of beautiful Lenten hymns. The chancel was bedecked with palms and Easter lilies.

As we joined the other worshippers, the pastor went to the pulpit and began to read the familiar Easter scripture that begins, "Very early in the morning, on the first day of the week . . ." and I began to envision myself in that garden. The message was especially poignant for me that Sunday in the lovely sanctuary. I felt a peace that remained with me for a long time.

The Easter breakfast was held in the annex in back of the church, so the smell of bacon and coffee did not detract from the flowers in the sanctuary. When the service was over, most of the congregation made their way toward the food. Silence gave way to chatter, and Louie was busy introducing me to people whose names I promptly forgot, when a hostess announced that the pastor had arrived and was ready to offer thanks for the food.

We found a couple of empty seats at a table nearby, across from a couple of Louie's friends. They shared memories of times spent with the Reyner boys in days past, and I discovered more about my future family as we enjoyed pleasant conversation along with our delicious meal.

After breakfast we decided to take a walk. It was a beautiful morning, and we needed some time alone before taking on the schedule for the rest of the day.

We were thankful for the time in Petoskey, but concerned about the trouble we had caused others in getting there. We both felt some responsibility for the breakdown of Freal's car; although he assured us that it was an old vehicle and would have had trouble no matter who was driving at the time.

We also had the problem of my return to Grand Rapids. "I can just take the bus." I said. "My dad can pick me up at the bus stop downtown when he gets out of work. I'm sure he wouldn't mind."

"I was thinking of the bus too, but I want to go with you. I could spend the night in Grand Rapids and go on the next day to Naperville to visit the college and register for classes."

I wasn't enthusiastic about traveling back by bus alone, and welcomed the possibility of his company. As he intended to go on to Illinois, and I would be with my family and friends in Grand Rapids for the remainder of my vacation, I decided to offer the use of my car for his trip. If he could return by the weekend, we could arrange for his trip back to Petoskey and I could return to my school on time.

There was no time for further discussion, as we were back at the church where people were arriving for the main Easter Sunday service. We found Louie's parents in the crowd and joined them in entering the sanctuary.

We had just taken our seats, when Freal's family arrived. When they saw us they came over to wish us a happy Easter. "Aren't you going to sing with the choir this morning?" Freal asked Louie. "We really could use another tenor."

Louie gave me a questioning look and I nodded my head in approval. When her family headed for the back of the church, Mrs. Reyner touched me on the hand and explained, "Freal and Mary are both in the choir, and Louis sings whenever he is here. The little girls are in Sunday school and the nursery. I hope you don't mind just sitting here with Daddy and me."

I assured her that I didn't mind at all and was glad to have their company.

The service was not like the quiet, meditative, sunrise service, but rather a joyous celebration of the Resurrection. The message dealt with the significance of the event and the effect it has made on civilization. The choir performed a hymn of praise that added to the spirit of the day. After the benediction a cheerful congregation left the church, greeting one another as they headed for home and Easter dinner.

As their car was still being repaired, Freal's family rode back to the Reyner house with Louie and me. We arrived to find the big kitchen table set for seven, and decorated for the occasion with little Easter baskets filled with jelly beans.

Little Nancy headed straight for the candy, but was warned that it was untouchable until after dinner.

Mary joined Mr. and Mrs. Reyner who were busy attending to the meal. I offered my help, but accepted their refusal. I was not accustomed to that kitchen; I would just be in the way. In no time at all a delicious roast beef dinner was on the table. Before the meal, Mr. Reyner offered an appropriate and sincere prayer of thanks.

The dinnertime conversation, which started with appreciation for the morning services, eventually evolved into an inquiry about my life. Realizing that I was almost a stranger in their midst, I overcame my shyness and answered questions about my family, my work, and my life. Finally everyone noticed that I had done a lot of talking, and very little eating, so the topic of conversation was changed to plans for the rest of the day.

Mrs. Reyner and little Nancy were each in need of a nap, so while they were resting, Mary and I helped the men clear away the dishes and straighten the kitchen. I was glad for the time to get better acquainted with this couple. Mary had a friendly, outgoing, personality and Freal kept us laughing with his droll sense of humor. I hoped we would be able to spend a lot of time with them in the future.

When we were finally ready to leave for Harbor Springs, we faced a transportation problem. Freal's car was in the garage, and Mr. Reyner's could not accommodate all of us. After some discussion, it was decided that we would take the truck. Mr. and Mrs. Reyner and the girls would ride in the cab, and Freal, Mary, Louis, and I on benches in back. Mrs. Reyner loaned me a headscarf and I wore my coat as protection from the wind; but from where I sat, directly behind the cab, it was hardly necessary.

There was little traffic that afternoon, and Mr. Reyner drove slowly, allowing me to get a view of the area. We rode through Bay View, an exclusive resort on the order of Chautauqua in New York; and along Little Traverse Bay, past the mansions in the community of Wequetonsing; until we arrived at Harbor Springs, a picturesque little village nestled between the bay on the south and steep hills on the north.

The town was a haven for tourists. Exclusive shops, boutiques, and restaurants lined the streets along the bay. At the end of the main street was an impressive white church with a tall steeple, topped by a shining gold cross that glistened in the afternoon sun. I was told that a residential school and orphanage was directly behind the church, but it wasn't visible from the road.

Marvin, Kathryn, and their family lived on a street at the top of the hill, from which they had a view of the village and bay below. When they saw the truck turn into the drive, they came out of the house to greet us. The weather was unseasonably warm, so we spent much of the afternoon outdoors; the adults on the porch, and the children running around in the yard.

Marvin, Louie's oldest brother, bore most resemblance to Louie. They both were tall and sturdy, with dark hair. Freal had smaller features, and fair hair and complexion. I thought all the brothers were handsome, though definitely different from one another.

After we had visited for an hour or more, Marvin asked if I had been to Harbor Point. I replied that I had been told the place was a summer resort for the very wealthy; a gated community where no motor vehicles were allowed.

"Well, the resort season doesn't begin until Memorial Day, and the gates are open. What do you say we drive out there and show Bev the view from the other side of the bay?" he asked the others.

Louie and I, along with Freal and Mary, agreed enthusiastically; while the children preferred to stay and continue their play, and the rest of the adults chose to stay with them.

"You go ahead and enjoy yourselves," Mr. Reyner said. "We have been to the Point many times."

Marvin drove with Louie and I in front, while Mary and Freal rode in the back seat. We headed down a curved road at a speed that was unsettling, but Marv knew the territory and nobody complained. He slowed down when we reached the road along the bay, and turned west. We passed the public bathing beach and came to a huge garage where, according to Marvin, residents of "the Point" left their cars to travel the rest of the distance to their homes in horse drawn carriages.

A high stone wall prohibited non-residents from a view of the point, and tall iron gates prohibited their entry. During the off-season, however, the gates were left open for snow removal, safety inspections, and any repairs that were necessary.

A sand dune and a copse of pine trees appeared as we went through the gates. There was no sign of habitation until we rounded a curve in the road. Then we caught sight of the huge mansions that gave the peninsula its reputation. Although they looked like expensive hotels, Marvin assured me that they were all single family dwellings; each valued at over a million dollars.

On the west side of the peninsula, manicured lawns led to the rocky shore of Lake Michigan; on the east, to the sandy beaches of the bay. At the point there was a lighthouse that invited sailors into a harbor that was second to none in the country.

After stopping to take a few pictures, we headed back to Harbor Springs and the supper that Kathryn had prepared for us. I had been told that she was an excellent cook, but was not prepared for the delicious spread that was on the table. While enjoying the baked ham and rolls, enhanced by homemade condiments and salads, we told of our visit to Harbor Point. When asked my opinion of the place, I probably surprised the others:

"Yes it is a beautiful place," I said, "but it seems a shame that those big, expensive homes are used by so few people for three months of the year, when there are people who have inadequate housing, or none at all."

I looked up to see Mr. Reyner nodding his head in agreement.

It was getting dark and the warm afternoon had given way to a cool evening when Marvin said, "It's too cold to ride back to Petoskey in the truck now. Why don't I take some of you in the car? I have room for Bev and Louie, and Freal's family too, if the kids ride on the laps.

Everyone agreed to that arrangement and, as Mrs. Reyner was quite tired, she and Mr. Reyner left directly to return to Petoskey. Mary and I helped Kathryn clear the table and put away the food before we too gathered up the sleepy children and our belongings and prepared to leave.

"How long will you be in the area?" Kathryn asked Louie and me. "We would love to get together again, if you have time."

"We plan to leave in the morning," Louie replied. "We should have more time when Beverly comes north again."

We thanked her for her hospitality and the wonderful meal; then all piled into the car for the return to Petoskey. The drive back seemed much shorter than our trip to Harbor Springs. Marvin was a fast driver and it was too dark to enjoy the scenery. By the time we arrived at their house the little girls were fast asleep, and didn't even notice when they were carried from the car to their beds.

Just around the corner at their grandparent's house, one small light was burning; indicating that they were already in bed. Marvin decided to not come in; so we thanked him for the ride and promised to see them soon.

We entered the house as quietly as possible and in a whisper I said, "It has been a wonderful Easter and I have enjoyed every moment of it: the church services, the family gatherings, the beautiful trip to Harbor Springs, the delicious meals . . ."

"I did too," he responded, because I was with you."

I rose early the next morning, and packed my bag before joining the others for breakfast. I had little to pack, but encountered a problem when I tried to fit my suit into my little suitcase. "I guess I'll just have to wear it," I decided.

Louis was surprised but pleased when I came to breakfast dressed so formally. "I have been wondering how to carry my sport coat," he said. "Now I think I'll just wear it."

Mr. Reyner was at the breakfast table, dressed for work and, although it was almost seven o'clock, he seemed in no hurry to leave. "Good morning, Beverly," he said. "I hope you slept well.

"Dad has offered to take us to the bus station in his truck," said Louie, "although I am afraid it will make him late for work."

"That is not a problem," Mr. Reyner assured us, "it makes up for the many days when I am early."

At eight o'clock, as a well-dressed couple, we boarded the bus for the long trip to Grand Rapids. The bus was nearly empty when it arrived in Petoskey, but several other people boarded before we left the city.

We stopped at four small towns before arriving in Kalkaska, where we had a fifteen minute layover. It was good to get out and enjoy some fresh air and exercise. We walked past the hotel, and marveled that only three days had passed since our short sojourn in the town.

Back on the bus, our conversation shifted from my impressions of the Petoskey area and the Reyner family to what we would do once we arrived in Grand Rapids. My plan was to call my father from the bus depot; certain that he would be glad to provide transportation to our house, where my mother would probably have dinner waiting. Louie was reluctant to impose, but I insisted that Dad would be offended if we hired a taxi and the bus was out of the question. Finally we agreed to make the call.

With that issue settled we turned to another that proved controversial. I understood that Louie had agreed to use my car for his trip to Naperville, but now he seemed to have reservations about doing so.

"I appreciate your offer, Honey," he said, "but after my experience with Freal's car I am uncomfortable borrowing again."

"But we will soon be married," I countered, "and the car will belong to both of us."

"I would like that to occur before I leave for Naperville," he replied. "You told me that you still owed your father four hundred dollars for the car. I have that much and more from my discharge allotment. I want to pay your father whatever you owe him, and then the car will be "ours". That is the only way I will feel comfortable using it for a long trip."

We debated the issue until we arrived in Grand Rapids and Dad picked us up at the bus station. We didn't mention it again until after dinner when Dad was relaxing in his easy chair, smoking his pipe. Louie broached the subject with the same argument that he had given me. Dad thought for several minutes before turning to me and saying, "How do you feel about this, Beverly? You know it isn't necessary to pay off the car now. You have made regular payments, and that is fine with me."

"We discussed it at length as we traveled," I replied, "I am all right with the idea, if this is what Louie wants to do."

After our discussion Dad offered to drive us out to the farm where we had left the car for the weekend. He asked about our trip and inquired after Louie's family as he drove.

The Duforts greeted us warmly, and offered coffee and cookies. Dad stayed to talk, but Louie and I thanked Ellen and left for a movie and some time alone before he left for Illinois in the morning.

Our house was small, with only three bedrooms. My parents' room was on the main floor, and we four girls shared the rooms upstairs, so Louie was relegated to the sofa in the living room. Mother had set out bedding before she retired and arranged the furniture to provide a modicum of privacy, but we decided to bid each other goodnight while in the car and on the front porch. It was actually goodbye, for he left for Naperville early the next morning with a peck and a promise to call.

I enjoyed the next few days with family and friends in Grand Rapids, but I missed my time with Louie. He called every evening with a record of his progress, but enrollment was taking longer than he expected due to some difficulty accessing service credits and completing an application for the G.I. Bill. He expected to return on Saturday in time for dinner, so I planned to make a special meal that night.

He arrived back in Grand Rapids later than expected due to tire trouble on the highway. He was able to drive as far as Benton Harbor, but by the time he arrived at a garage the tire was beyond repair. While he waited for the dealer to locate another, he went to a little restaurant across the street and had supper. He was upset with the delay and the need to purchase a tire, and I was equally upset with his late arrival, although I knew it couldn't be helped. The special meal I had prepared for him had become a treat for the dog.

After spending some time with my family we decided to walk down to an ice-cream parlor a few blocks away; we needed some exercise and time alone to talk. Our spirits revived as he took my hand and we were able to laugh about the first meal I had prepared for him being dinner for the dog! Over dessert we shared the events of the last few days; then we went back home for a night of rest, he on the sofa and I upstairs with my sisters.

The next day was Sunday. We went to the church where we had first met and were greeted warmly by many old friends and the pastor, who was delighted to learn that Louie was planning to enter the ministry. We lingered after the service until most of the congregation had left. We declined invitations to dinner with the explanation that we had to get on the road if we were to reach our destinations before dark.

Louie drove as far as Cadillac where we stopped for dinner. Having enjoyed our meals at "Johnie's Restaurant", we decided to eat there again. The food was excellent, but the thought of another separation affected our appetites.

"It won't be long until Memorial Day, Louie said, and we can be together for another long weekend. The Hamiltons have invited me to stay at their house, but they know I will want to spend the time with you. Until then we each have a busy schedule. I hope to begin a new job as radio announcer, and you will be finishing your first year of teaching."

We said goodbye out in the parking lot. I waited until he had a ride and was headed north before I left to go back to the farm, my second home.

# CHAPTER 13

## Year One Ends

It was a lonely drive from Cadillac to Algoma Township, but I relieved my melancholy by recalling the pleasant experiences of the past week. My future in-laws accepted me as family, and I had become acquainted with a beautiful part of the state that was totally unlike the area where I had grown up. I had enjoyed a wonderful Easter vacation, but now it was time to get back to work.

It was growing dark as I approached the little town of Rockford; so I decided to avoid the country roads at night and turned west on Thirteen Mile Road. It was paved, well traveled, and intersected directly with Grange Road which led to the farm.

The sky was clear, and soon I was able see the yard light that seemed to welcome me back. As I turned into the drive, Laddie, the collie dog barked his welcome, and Harry came to the door to ask if I needed any help with my luggage. I entered the kitchen, where Ellen met me and asked if I would like some supper. Bob and Lorraine greeted me from the living room and inquired about my trip. I was home again, with my wonderful second family.

Although I wasn't hungry, Ellen insisted that I have a bowl of popcorn and an apple, the usual Sunday evening fare with the Dufort family. They turned off the television so they could hear all about Louie's family and the places we had visited while up north. They were especially interested in hearing about Harbor Point.

Soon I was beginning to feel the effect of my long day and the two hundred mile road trip. My eyes were getting heavy, and I had trouble suppressing a yawn. Ellen, aware of my condition, excused me from the conversation. "Bev looks like she is going to fall asleep in that chair. I think we better save the rest of her story for another time."

Before long I was back in the familiar, comfortable, bed that had been my nightly retreat for over nine months. I felt safe and secure listening to the muffled sounds of the television and quiet conversation from downstairs. In no time at all I was sound asleep.

I awoke early the following morning, feeling refreshed and eager to begin my day. Ellen prepared a big breakfast, suitable for hungry farmers. It was delicious, and more than I needed, but I ate it all. Then I thanked her, gave her a hug, and went out the door. She called to me before I reached the car. She was holding a brown paper bag that held my lunch.

We both knew I would appreciate it after a busy morning with the children.

The day was sunny and bright, but a cool wind made me thankful for my warm coat. I arrived at the school expecting to enter a cool classroom, but to my surprise someone had been there earlier, for the room was comfortable. It had also received a thorough cleaning; the bathrooms were immaculate and the floors and desktops fairly shone.

On my desk was a large envelope from the Kent County Board of Education. I knew its contents before I opened it. It held the results of the achievement tests that I had administered in March. I opened the package with some anxiety, knowing that inside were not only evaluations of the students, but also of me as their teacher.

The packet contained over a dozen pages. The first was a list of the students who had taken the test and the grade level at which they had performed in each area. I studied the material carefully, and was pleased that most of my students were above average. Many tested above grade level in all areas. Others had trouble with certain subjects, but had performed well enough on others that there was no reason to retain anyone.

Before long the children arrived, their cheeks red from wind. They were happy to come inside where it was warm and friends were gathering. I caught snippets of conversation from the cacophony around me, enough to know that most of them had enjoyed their vacation. Several asked about my trip, and I gave the simple reply, "I had a wonderful time."

I didn't need to ring the bell, for by eight-thirty they were all in their seats and ready to begin the day. We began with the now familiar opening exercises, followed by my customary message to the children.

"From what I heard this morning, I think that most of you enjoyed your vacation. So did I, but now we must get back to work, for we have only six weeks left in this school year."

Holding up the packet of tests, I continued, "This material was on my desk when I arrived this morning. It contains the results of your achievement tests, and I want you to know that I am very proud of you. After lunch, while you are working on your regular assignments, I will call you to my desk, one at a time. Together we will go over your test results and decide where you should concentrate your study for the rest of the year. Now we will continue our regular schedule, and I will meet with the kindergarten first."

The children around the table had changed from the shy little ones with the quiet voices that greeted me each morning in September. They had grown in every way: physically, they were taller and more robust; mentally, they could already read and write simple sentences and perform minor math functions; and emotionally, they had overcome feelings of insecurity. In fact, at that moment they were clamoring to be first to tell of their vacation activities.

While they were talking I wrote some of the words they were using on sheets of paper. After everyone had a chance to share, I gave them each a list of the more difficult words, and asked them to write about their vacations. After they were finished, they were to draw a picture to illustrate their story.

It was a new endeavor, but I knew it was within their capabilities. However, I asked some of my eighth grade students to give help where needed while I went on to the first grade class.

We chatted a little about their vacations before they took turns reading orally from their first grade reader, which had grown more difficult and interesting as it progressed. They would soon be done with that book; then I would encourage them to read books of their own choosing, and be able to share the stories with the class.

Their writing assignment was the same as the kindergarten, but could be fiction if they chose. If necessary they could ask an older student how to spell a difficult word. They too were to draw pictures to accompany their stories.

I went from class to class all morning, pausing only for recess. As I met with each, I measured their progress and determined what should be accomplished in the waning school year.

During recess children came to my desk to examine the items I had purchased from the gift store in Petoskey. They were especially impressed with the tepee made of deerskin. I let them handle it and feel the soft leather. I explained that, although many Indians still lived in that area, they no longer lived like their ancestors hundreds of years before. Now they had houses like ours. Several of the boys thought it would be more fun to live in a tepee.

The older children, girls especially, wondered what my boyfriend and I did in Petoskey. I told them that I had met his family and visited many beautiful places in the area. The Holden girls wondered if he had liked my new suit. I answered in the affirmative, and said that I not only wore it on Easter, but also on the trip back home, and received many compliments.

As promised, I spent the afternoon with the older children individually, reviewing test scores and identifying areas where more effort was required. Some of the students, who scored above grade level on the math test and had finished the assignments in their books, chose to attempt math at the next higher grade level. Those who were above grade level in reading could choose their books, with my supervision, of course. Several eighth graders volunteered to read to the little children or help them with their lessons.

The days were getting warmer, and the children loved to be outdoors, so I tried to include learning activities that could get them out of the classroom. One morning, after a rain, the little children found earthworms on the playground. We stayed outdoors and enjoyed a little science lesson. They all knew that the worm was good for fishing, but were surprised to learn how beneficial it is to farmers and gardeners. We located earthworm burrows near the school, and I explained how they enrich the soil.

It turned out to be a beautiful day and I decided that the older children deserved time outdoors also. We had little science equipment, but there was a beautiful wood just across the road. After recess we left the schoolhouse to look for signs of life among the trees.

One of our first discoveries was a group of Jack-in-the-Pulpit plants. The students were intrigued by the little flower covered with an umbrella-like leaf. Some wanted to pick the flowers or dig up the plants to replant at home. I explained that they we could do neither because it was against the law to do so. The Jack-in-the Pulpit was becoming very rare, and was now labeled one of the endangered species.

We found many other signs of life that were interesting but not so rare, including nests of birds and squirrels. We marveled at the variety of construction and decided to search the encyclopedias back in the classroom to determine the species that built the most unusual structures.

We also found the footprints of several animals. The deer and raccoon were easy to identify, but others were less familiar. Was it the print of a fox or a small dog? Some of the boys were determined to find out.

We headed back to the school with just enough time to do some research or draw pictures of some of the things we saw on our little expedition.

April gave way to May, and the students were busy working on their individual assignments or activities of their choice. As I turned the calendar to the new month, I told the children of the significance of May first to people around the world, and how it had been celebrated in our own country with Maypoles and May baskets. Some of the children wanted to make baskets, and I provided materials and directions, while several of the older children offered assistance where necessary. A few wildflowers (weeds) were growing along the perimeters of the schoolyard, and the younger children spent their recess trying to assemble a suitable bouquet.

As more and more students completed their assignments, they were left with free time. Although some would have preferred to spend it all on the playground engaged in a lively game of ball, I decided to apply some time each day to familiarize them with the classics in literature. The kindergarten enjoyed a carefully selected story time and, after the lunch recess, the rest of the children listened as I read from the classics and some of the popular newer books. While I read, I was able to define unfamiliar words or concepts so that all the children could understand the stories.

Mothers Day afforded another diversion for the children, as they used their talents and a variety of art material to produce unique cards and gifts for their mothers. Except for the youngest children, the students were left to their own designs, and I was amazed at the creativity they displayed.

As the final weeks of the school year approached I was filled with a variety of emotions. Although I would miss the children, I expected to see them again in the fall; that is all except the eighth-graders.

One day, as I watched those students working quietly at their desks, I realized how much they had contributed to my first year of teaching. Tom, in his quiet way, set the standard of behavior for the school and served as a mentor to the younger children; Ruth had become a very valuable, if unpaid, teacher's aide; Leo not only was an excellent janitor, but his happy disposition and carefree spirit brightened even a cloudy day; and Patsy, with her sweet personality, was a friend to everyone. These four had become an important part of my life, and I would certainly miss them.

If they had any regret of leaving the school that had been not only their institution of learning but their social center for as many as nine years, it wasn't evident in the final weeks of the school year. Exciting events were taking place; there was no time for reminiscing.

A day was set aside when the eighth grade students from all the country schools in the township were to visit Rockford or Sparta High School for orientation and registration for the fall semester. Tom, Leo, Ruth, and Patsy came to school that morning dressed for the occasion and excited. At shortly after nine the yellow school bus arrived; a horn sounded and our prospective high school students were out the door.

The room seemed smaller without them, but I was surprised at how the remaining students filled the void, assuming the leadership roles without introduction or fanfare.

It was shortly after three when the bus returned. Leo was the first one in the door. He was exuberant! "Miss Haskins," he said in a loud voice. "They signed me up for algebra!"

The other three were comparing their class schedules, excited when they found a class they had in common. I imagined how difficult it could be for them in the fall to be in groups of total strangers.

Graduation was held in the Grange Hall, where I had made my commitment and signed my contract to become a teacher. As I watched my students go forward to receive their diplomas, I knew that I had made the right choice. No parent could have been more proud of her children.

Each year the graduates from the Algoma Township Schools were rewarded with a bus trip to the Upper Peninsula. This year I was invited to go along as one of the counselors. I recalled my high school senior trip and wondered what mischief this group of young teens could devise. As it turned out, I had no reason to be concerned.

On the morning of our departure I waited with my four students until Marvin Jewell, the township school bus driver, custodian, and all around handyman came down the road. His home was about a half mile from the school so ours was his first stop. He took our luggage, put it in the back of the bus, and welcomed us aboard with a big smile.

"You can have your choice of the seats this morning," he said. "I'll be stopping at the other schools before we head north, but that shouldn't take long. I hope you all used the rest rooms before you got on the bus."

Everyone answered in the affirmative so Marvin started the engine, and we were on our way.

We stopped at three or four other schools and took on passengers, both students and teachers. I was glad to see my friends Lois and Sue from Chalmers, our neighboring school, and greeted them enthusiastically. The other adults, teachers also I presumed, looked familiar but I did not know their names and no one introduced us. At our last stop, Lois moved to allow a student to sit with her friend, and sat in the empty seat beside me.

I was glad for her company, for although I was finally comfortable in my role as teacher, I had never served as a chaperone and had no clue as to what was expected of me.

Unlike me, Lois exuded complete confidence. She had a year of practice teaching before graduating from Western Michigan University, and I presumed she had been on school trips before. "Just relax and enjoy yourself, and keep an eye on your own kids," she said. "The other teachers are doing the same. If you see a kid who is in trouble, either one of yours or someone else's, try to solve the problem, that's all."

"Exactly where are we going, and what will we do when we get there?" I asked. "I haven't seen a map or an agenda."

"Neither have I," she replied with a laugh. "I understand that we're going to a place called Sugar Island, somewhere in the Upper Peninsula. Marvin knows where it is, and perhaps some of the other teachers. I think they have been there before."

"According to Marvin we will stop for lunch in Petoskey, go on to Sugar Island in the afternoon and return to Saint Ignace for dinner. I understand reservations have been made at a restaurant with an attached gift shop where the kids can buy souvenirs. The motel where we will be staying has two wings, one to accommodate the boys, the other the girls. There is also a small conference room with tables, where we can get together after dinner and play table games."

"Where did you get all that information?" I asked.

"Remember, our school is right across the street from the general store. I go over there almost every day. I hear a lot of news, and I'm not afraid to ask questions."

"Thanks for filling me in. I feel a lot better, knowing what's going on. I don't know about the destination, but I think the trip is a good idea. Right now my kids are sitting together, talking to one another. Hopefully, by the time we return they will be sitting with new friends. It should help in their adjustment to high school."

"I agree," she responded, "and some of these kids have been no farther from home than Rockford or Sparta, except possibly for a rare trip to Grand Rapids. This is a real journey for them."

We arrived in Petoskey shortly before noon and stopped at a little restaurant on the highway called Wimpy's. I was in familiar territory, but had never been inside this establishment. It was essentially a fast food place, connected to a gas station with a rest room.

After a few directions from Marvin, the kids hurried off the bus; some headed for the restaurant, others to the gas station next door. Lois and I didn't leave until we were sure that all of the children were headed in the right direction. In about an hour, after everyone had finished their lunch and used the restrooms, we were on the road again.

Before long we arrived in Mackinaw City, where we boarded the ferry for the short trip across the Straights of Mackinaw to the Upper Peninsula. Many of the kids had never been on anything larger than a rowboat on a small inland lake, and found the experience somewhat daunting; but with a little coaxing, we were able to get everyone on board. The water was a little choppy and I have a tendency toward motion sickness, so I opted to sit outside on the deck. It wasn't long before I had plenty of company.

On the next segment of the trip I sat with Patsy Becker. She was sitting alone when I boarded the bus and beckoned me to the seat beside her. I appreciated the invitation to join her. She was a quiet girl, and seldom talked about herself, so I was glad for the opportunity to become better acquainted.

She told me of her feelings of insecurity when she thought of going from her one room school to high school, and the problem of making new friends. It was so easy for Ruth; she had already met a new friend and was sitting with her; but Patsy was shy and found it hard to speak to strangers.

"Patsy," I said, "I'm sure there are people right here on the bus who feel just like you do. When we stop, look around you. I'm sure you will see someone standing alone. Go up to that person and introduce yourself and ask her some simple questions about herself. Then tell her a little about yourself. It really isn't so hard. You are a pretty girl with a sweet personality; I'm sure you will have plenty of friends when school starts in the fall."

We had been deep in conversation, and I had paid no attention to where we were headed until the bus was bouncing over ruts on a dirt road that was heavily wooded on both sides. If we had crossed a bridge and were now on an island I hadn't noticed; my mind was on other matters. However, we certainly were in a remote area. There was no room for another vehicle to pass; the road was so narrow that low branches occasionally brushed the side of the bus. I prayed that we were on the right road, as there was nowhere to turn around.

Suddenly we came to a large clearing with a log house in the middle, and several outbuildings nearby. Beside one of the buildings, in a fenced area, was the strangest looking dog I had ever seen. He was built like a bear, but had a long tail and ears like retriever.

When he saw the bus arrive the owner of the place came out to greet us. "Stay away from the dog!" he yelled, when he saw some of the kids headed that way. "He's a one family dog and he doesn't like strangers."

"What kind of dog is he?" I asked, my curiosity getting the best of me.

"Don't rightly know," he replied. "His mother was a black lab. We were surprised when she became pregnant. As far as we knew there wasn't another dog on this island. She had only the one pup, that one over there," he said, as he pointed to the dog behind the fence. "She died birthing him."

The owner appeared to be Indian, and from all appearances we were at a fish camp. Marvin and the owner seemed to be old friends, as they led the kids around the property, showing them the boats, equipment and even some mounted fish of considerable size.

The boys were interested in everything they saw, but some of the girls held back, offended by the smell and not wanting to get dirt on their new white sneakers. My father was an avid fisherman, so I had my fill of fish and fish stories. I spent the time with the girls in the clean white shoes. We stayed at the camp for over an hour; then boarded the bus and headed back to St. Ignace.

By the time we arrived at the restaurant everyone was hungry and ready to get off the bus. The kids hurried inside and were looking at the menus when I entered with the rest of the adults. I was pleased to see my students sitting with kids from other schools. They were talking and laughing together like old friends.

It was a humble little restaurant, with a limited menu, but the food was good and plentiful. The kids ate quickly; then hurried off to the gift shop. The rest of us lingered over coffee and homemade desserts.

I looked up from the table and was surprised to see Tom Teesdale leaving the restaurant. I excused myself and hurried after him, afraid that he was ill or that something had happened to upset him. I called to him, and he waited until I reached his side. "Tom," I said in a worried voice, "what's the matter; where are you going?"

"I'm going over to the motel," he answered. "It's my bedtime."

With that he left me and continued down the road in the direction of the motel.

I went back to the restaurant and told Marvin what had occurred, thinking that he might go over to check on Tom. Instead he just laughed and said, "Don't worry about Tommy. He knows how to take care of himself. He probably was up at four-thirty helping with the chores and he's tired. He knows where his bed is. He'll be all right."

After the adults had finished their coffee and the kids their shopping, everyone headed for the little conference room in the motel. We unloaded the games and snacks from the bus and settled down for a little party. The teachers gathered around one table and played cards, while the kids played table games around the other tables in the room. The room was noisy with talking, laughing, and the rustling bags of popcorn and chips.

The card game meanwhile was getting intense and no one noticed how quiet the room had become, until someone looked around and said, "Where are the kids!"

We hurried to our assigned quarters, each of which contained three bunks and a single bed for the teacher. I checked the beds in my room. Each one was filled with a girl who was either asleep or pretending to be.

We returned to the conference room and laughed as we picked up the papers and put the games and leftover treats back in the bus. If the kids had decided to play a trick on us, they certainly had succeeded!

I went back to my quarters and as I was preparing for bed I checked my watch. It was ten o'clock.

The following morning the girls woke early; full of energy and bubbling with excitement. They were now comfortable with each other, and I enjoyed listening to their happy banter. However, when a couple pillows sailed across the room, I had to intervene. We didn't have time to pluck feathers from the beds, furniture and floors, not to mention the open suitcases. It was time for breakfast and another long day.

We lingered over the meal. No one seemed anxious to get back on the bus for the trip home. Marvin was laying out the schedule for the day, but only the teachers were listening. The kids were talking about more important things, like how they would spend the summer vacation and what subjects they would take when school resumed in the fall.

Finally Marvin stood and announced in a loud voice that the bus would be loading in ten minutes, and anyone who wanted to visit the gift shop or the rest room should do so immediately.

The kids arrived at the designated place on time. They were chattering and laughing as they boarded the bus and chose their seats. By the time I got on, the only seat available was beside another teacher. I didn't know her very well, and was glad for the opportunity to get better acquainted. I was also pleased that the kids were all sitting with a friend.

We returned to the Lower Peninsula on the ferry. The water was fairly calm, and the kids enjoyed walking around and enjoying the vista from various places on the boat. The captain pointed out some important sights like Mackinac Island and places where ships had gone down.

We stopped for lunch at a Mom and Pop restaurant south of Petoskey. It had a service station next door where

Marvin was able to buy gas and check the oil and tires. By the time he came into the restaurant, most of the kids had placed their orders. "Eat your fill," he said in a loud voice. "We won't be making another stop until we're home."

By the time we reached Cadillac, the sun was setting. Some of the kids were getting hungry, so Lois and Sue retrieved the snacks from the night before and passed them up and down the aisles. They were gone in no time.

Then Lois, who had a good loud voice, led the whole group in some camp-style songs that almost everyone knew. Those who couldn't sing well, sang loud; and everyone seemed in a joyful mood as we began to enter familiar territory.

Before long we were back in Algoma Township. Marvin dropped the kids off at their homes. As I said goodbye to my kids for the last time, I wanted to hug them and tell them that I would miss them, but of course I didn't. After all, they were teenagers now.

# CHAPTER 14

## Summer Vacation

Memorial Day marked the start of a very busy summer. Louie came to Grand Rapids as promised, and we had an enjoyable holiday weekend that included a day at the beach in Grand Haven. However, our brief vacation ended the following day when he returned to Petoskey to begin his new job as announcer for the local radio station, and I enrolled in two summer courses at Calvin College.

To cover college costs and provide some discretionary income I reapplied for work at Steketees' Department Store. I was pleased when I was hired with a schedule that accommodated my Calvin program, but there was little time for leisure activities, and Louie and I found our communication was again limited to letters and phone calls.

Fortunately, Independence Day that year fell on Saturday. Louie's parents had invited me to their home for the holiday weekend, and I looked forward to spending a few days with my fiancé in beautiful northern Michigan.

The store closed on Friday at noon to accommodate travelers who were heading to their holiday destinations. I planned to join the crowd going north as soon as possible. After a quick stop at home to grab a bite to eat and pick up my luggage, I was on my way.

As I approached the highway I could see traffic backed up for over a mile. Fortunately I was now familiar with an alternate route, the one I took to Algoma Township every week. I reversed direction and headed back to Alpine Avenue for an easy trip to Rockford, where I was able to get on the highway and join the parade.

The four lane highway that led out of Grand Rapids had narrowed to two, and the frustratingly slow traffic stopped frequently, as cars entered or left the road. A few, with steam escaping from under the hood, headed for the shoulder. Louie would have stopped to offer assistance, but I just kept my place in line and continued on my slow journey. Our little Ford was performing well, and I hoped to make Cadillac by supper time.

It was after seven when I arrived at Johnie's Restaurant. To save time, I took a seat at the counter and ordered soup. The food was delicious, but I didn't linger to savor it. There was a phone on the wall at the back of the establishment and I stopped to call Louie and tell him that I was running late. Then I headed back to the car to resume my trip north.

Traffic was lighter as I left Cadillac and headed for Petoskey, but it was a lonely trip, so I amused myself by reciting poetry or singing old, familiar songs. With no one listening, it didn't matter if I was out of tune.

By the time I arrived in Kalkaska it was dark, but the lights of the little town encouraged me to go on. There was still some traffic ahead and behind me, giving me a sense of security.

I passed through several little towns before coming to the high hill leading into Petoskey. From there the lights of the city shone like diamonds around the dark water of the bay.

I turned off the highway onto Sheridan Street and continued up the hill to the Reyner home. Louie saw the car turn into the drive and came out to greet me with a big hug. He took my bag and led me inside, where his parents were anxiously awaiting my arrival. They asked about my trip, and commiserated over the heavy traffic and delays that had been the cause of my tardiness and frustration.

"You must be hungry," said Mrs. Reyner, who was heading for the kitchen. I informed her that I had stopped in Cadillac, and couldn't eat another bite. However, I did accept her offer of lemonade. She went to the kitchen, and returned to the living room carrying a tray with a glass of the cool beverage for each of us.

Eventually our conversation included plans for the weekend. Louie turned to me with a look of disappointment. "I had planned to take you to the Doris Day movie at the theatre tonight, followed by ice-cream at the Arcadia, but the show is half over by now. Then he added, "The restaurant is still open for dessert, if you'd care to go."

I declined as graciously as I could, admitting that, at the time, I had no desire to get back in the car, even for ice-cream. "Perhaps you could give me a rain-check for tomorrow night," I said with a smile.

"I'm afraid there will be no time for either ice-cream or movie tomorrow," he replied. Then he surprised me with an agenda that allowed little time for us to be alone. "Marvin and Katie have asked us to join them for a cookout on the beach north of Harbor Springs tomorrow night, and the folks are planning a picnic with Freal's family in the afternoon; we're included, of course. There is even a parade in the morning, if you're interested."

"It sounds like a busy day to me," I said with a sigh.

Mr. Reyner turned to me with a look of concern. "Beverly, I know that you plan to head south again on Sunday, but I hope you will consider staying another day. You need a day of rest. The traffic could be as heavy on your return trip as it was today, and you will begin your work week exhausted rather than refreshed from your vacation. I've seen it happen all too often."

I promised to consider his sound advice, and see what could be arranged, although I knew there was no way to contact my employer before Monday morning.

After a night of rest, I felt ready to enjoy the holiday. Louie and I had a breakfast of cold cereal before walking down the hill to Mitchell Street. We joined the crowd in front of the J.C. Penney Store and waited for the annual Independence Day parade to begin.

It wasn't long before the high school band came down the street, followed by decorated vehicles and floats from practically every organization in town. Flags were hung from lamp posts and carried by the boy and girl scouts who marched by. It was a patriotic celebration of which the city could be proud.

After the last unit had passed and the band was only an echo in the distance, we crossed the street and headed for a little soda fountain located behind the Visitors' Center on the corner. We bought a couple bottles of pop, and sat on a bench in the park to relax and cool off before walking back up the hill to the Reyner house.

Refreshed by the by the rest and cool beverage, we started the climb up Howard Street. On the way, Louie described Jones' Landing where our picnic lunch was to be held. "It is a secluded little beach on Walloon Lake, owned by friends who attend our church," he said. "There are no public facilities, so we take care of our needs before leaving home and wear our swimsuits under our clothes."

We arrived at their home to find Mr. and Mrs. Reyner ready to leave for the lake. Their picnic basket and thermos jug of lemonade were already in the trunk of their car. They waited patiently as we went inside and changed our clothes, taking a couple of towels from the bathroom as we left.

On the Charlevoix Road, about eight miles west of Petoskey, was a sign pointing to Jones' Landing. We turned south and followed the road for about a mile before it came to an abrupt end at the very edge of beautiful Walloon Lake.

Mr. Reyner parked the car in a shady spot under a tree, and Louie and I helped to unload the picnic supplies. We waved to Freal and his family, who were already in the water.

Louie's father was gathering wood for a bonfire, when he said, with a big smile, "It is going to take a while to get a fire hot enough roast the wieners, so why don't you young folks get in the water and cool off while I play Boy Scout."

He didn't seem to need our assistance, so after shedding our jeans and shirts we joined Freal, Mary, and the girls, who were enjoying themselves in the cool, clear lake. We swam and played in the water for nearly an hour, until Mr. Reyner called to announce that dinner was ready.

A table cloth had been spread on a grassy spot under a tree. It held an appetizing assortment of picnic foods, including potato salad, baked beans, fruit, and a variety of condiments. We roasted wieners over the hot coals of the bonfire until they were just the way we liked them. We were hungry after our refreshing swim, and everyone ate heartily.

By mid-afternoon the girls were getting sleepy. We took one last dip in the lake before heading back to Petoskey.

There was just time to change our clothes and relax a bit before leaving for the next event of the day, a cookout on the beach at Harbor Springs. Louie advised me to take a jacket, as an evening at Lake Michigan could be cool. I did as he suggested, although I thought it would certainly be unnecessary; after all, it was July, and weather was still hot and humid when we left the house.

It's been said that the population of Petoskey doubles in the summer, and it certainly appeared to be the case as we drove through town. The streets and sidewalks were crowded and pedestrians, knowing they had right of way, darted into traffic from between parked cars.

Around Bay View and the state park the traffic was bumper to bumper. I thought of the trip back to Grand Rapids and considered heeding Mr. Reyner's advice to wait until Monday for my return.

We arrived at Katie and Marvin's a little later than planned, but they didn't seem to mind. The children were at their grandmother's house, enjoying the company of cousins who had come north for the holiday; so the house was peaceful and quiet.

"There is a secluded place on the beach north of town where you can see fireworks from both Harbor Springs and Petoskey," Kate said, as we headed toward their car. We will have to park along the highway and climb over a little dune to get there, but the view is worth it."

It was a short drive to the site she had described. Marvin parked the car well off the road, and we all helped to carry the supplies down to the beach. It was getting late, and we were hungry, so we decided to eat first and explore the beach later.

We cooked hamburgers and sweet corn on a small charcoal grill that Marvin had brought along for the occasion. Katie's salad and dessert added the finishing touches to a delicious meal.

After supper we walked along the shore and while the men collected driftwood for a bonfire Katie and I looked for Petoskey stones, little fossils that had value more for souvenirs of the area than money; although some local merchants polished them and made jewelry which they sold to tourists.

As the sun began to set in the west, we were treated to a beautiful sunset. However, it was accompanied by a cool wind that made us scurry for our jackets that were still in the car. Later, the men made a big bonfire which we enjoyed as we sat on blankets and watched the fireworks.

The wind picked up and our fire died down before the display came to an end. We were wrapped in blankets, waiting for the grand finale, when we felt the first raindrops. As quickly as possible we gathered up our belongings and headed for the car. Atop the dune, we looked back to see showers of fireworks from two cities falling like comets into the bay.

Back at their home, Marvin and Katie declined our offer to carry some of the picnic supplies inside. "Not in this rain," said Marvin. "We will leave them in the trunk until morning when the boys can help."

We thanked them for delightful evening before we all dashed through the downpour; they toward their door and we toward our vehicle.

The rain beat a staccato on the roof of the car, while the wipers responded in legato. The rhythm was soothing, and I was nearly asleep when Louie suddenly hit the brakes, narrowly avoiding a deer that darted across the road ahead. I was alert for the rest of the trip.

By the time he pulled into the drive, the rain was coming down in torrents. We were glad for the light above the back door that shone like a beacon in the storm. He turned off the ignition and we sat in the car for a few minutes waiting for the rain to abate. When that didn't happen, we headed for the door; which, thankfully, had not been locked for the night.

We didn't linger in the hall but, after a quick goodnight kiss, hurried to the bedrooms to shed our damp clothing and crawl into our nice warm beds. I fell asleep listening to the rain beating against the windows.

I woke to a grey morning. The storm of the night before had become a light drizzle. I was in no hurry to get up and lay there thinking of the trip back to Grand Rapids. I felt guilty missing a day of work, but Mr. Reyner was right,

I would be too tired to do a good job on Monday if I left Petoskey that day.

It rained intermittently all day. We went to church in the morning, but stayed indoors for the rest of the day. After dinner, while his mother was resting and his father writing letters, Louie and I completed our plans for the summer.

With our busy schedules, we figured that our next opportunity to be together was the last week in August, when Louie planned to move to Naperville, Illinois. He intended to get a ride as far as Grand Rapids and use our car for the rest of the trip. He would return on the weekend, as my new school year was to begin the day after Labor Day. We had about six weeks to work out the details of our plan; relying again on letters and phone calls. "Did any couple have a more irregular courtship?" I wondered.

By evening the rain had stopped, so we decided to go out for a bite to eat. Unlike the day before, the air was cool and we were glad for the jackets that had dried overnight. We drove through the town which was practically deserted and past Bay View where most of the cars were parked around the Bay View Inn. It appeared that the area had been evacuated due to the storm.

Louie laughed at my observation. "This is typical of resort areas," he said. "Most of the cars that were here yesterday are on the highways headed south; about where you would be had you left today."

We stopped at a little sandwich shop north of Bay View. Service was excellent, as there were few customers in the place. During the meal we concentrated on small talk, having covered the weightier matters earlier. Neither of us wanted to dwell on the long separation ahead.

On the way home Louie stopped at a scenic lookout, where we watched the sun set over Little Traverse Bay. "It's called the "Million Dollar Sunset," he said; "a real advertising asset for the Chamber of Commerce."

We stayed until it was dark and the lights on the pier reflected on the dark water. "I hate to leave, but I think we should go now," I said. "You have to work in the morning, and I want to leave for Grand Rapids as early as possible."

The streetlights were on and a few people were about as we drove back through town and up the hill to the Louie's home. His parents were at the kitchen table, enjoying popcorn and lemonade. They invited us to join them but, thinking of the long drive back to Grand Rapids, I excused myself and headed for bed. Although I was tired, I lay awake for a long time with countless thoughts going through my mind.

I awoke early the next morning. The sun was shining with the promise of a beautiful day. Anxious to be on my way, I declined their invitation to breakfast, promising Mr. and Mrs. Reyner that I would be stopping along the road to call my boss and get a bite to eat. I thanked them for their generous hospitality, and was about to leave when Louie appeared. He took my bag and walked with me to the car.

"Drive carefully and call me when you get home," he said. Then, after a big hug and kiss, added, "I love you."

"I love you, too." I responded. Then I started the engine and backed out of the driveway to begin my long trip back to Grand Rapids.

I made two stops along the way; first at a little restaurant in Kalkaska where I called my boss. His reply surprised me. "Thank you for calling," he said, "but you need not be concerned. We don't expect to be very busy on the day after the holiday weekend. Just drive carefully and we will see you tomorrow morning." With that in mind, I took a seat and ordered the breakfast special; bacon, eggs, and toast, that along with a cup of coffee satisfied my hunger for the rest of the trip.

My second stop was the farm. I arrived in mid-afternoon, when Ellen was busy writing letters. She stopped what she was doing and welcomed me with a big hug. She invited me to join her at the kitchen table and have a piece of pie that was fresh from the oven and intended for the evening meal. No one rejected Ellen's baked goods, and I was no exception. I enjoyed the pie with a cold glass of milk as I told her of my weekend up north.

When I asked about her holiday, she replied, "It was nothing out of the ordinary, except my sister Olga came for a visit on Sunday. Bob and Harry were busy with the usual chores and Lorraine and your sister Betty spent much of the weekend planning their trip to Bermuda."

That news surprised me. I knew that they had become friends, but I didn't know they were ready to take a long trip together. I was pleased with the concept of strengthening ties between my biological and foster families.

We eventually got around to the real reason for my visit, the possibility and conditions of spending another school year with this wonderful family. Ellen seemed surprised that I thought it necessary to inquire. "Of course," she replied emphatically. "We just expected you to return; why, you are just part of the family now."

"I was hoping that would be your reply, but didn't want to take anything for granted. It would be terrible to arrive at your doorstep, suitcase in hand, and find that the room was already taken," I said with a laugh.

"That would never happen," she replied tenderly. "By the way, before you leave would you please call Freeman Teasdale? He's been trying to get in touch with you. I think he wants to talk about your contract."

I called from the phone in the dining room, and returned to the kitchen with the result. "He would like me to meet him at the school in fifteen minutes. He wants to review a contract for the 1953-1954 school year. It shouldn't take long; I expect to sign."

As I prepared to leave for my meeting, I gave Ellen a big hug and said, "I am so glad to know that I am welcome here for another year. This has become my second home."

"Now don't wait until school starts to come back," she said, as I went out the door and headed for the car.

Mr. Teesdale was at the school when I arrived. He gave me a friendly greeting and motioned to the contract that was on the teacher desk. "Why don't you sit down and read it, and I will try to answer any questions you might have. You will notice there is a raise in salary this year. If you agree with the terms, just sign on the bottom line."

The contract was a duplicate of the year before, except for the raise which was two hundred dollars. I thanked him for the increase and agreed to be ready for school to begin the day after Labor Day at eight-thirty. With that, we shook hands and went out the door. The whole procedure took about ten minutes.

For the trip back to Grand Rapids, I chose the route I used when I signed my first contract over a year before. I smiled, remembering how intimidated I had felt at the prospect of teaching eight grades and kindergarten in a country school that I knew nothing about. Now I could sign a contract without hesitation and look forward to my return to the classroom. I was no longer the timid girl who had first traveled this road.

I arrived home less than an hour later, and received a warm welcome from my family. They were just sitting down to dinner, and invited me to join them. They asked about my trip, and I told them about the exhausting journey north and my decision to stay in Petoskey another day, which they agreed was the wise choice.

As we enjoyed our meal, I learned about the family holiday. They had the benefit of a weekend of good weather, which provided the backdrop for the annual Haskins family reunion at Long Lake. The event was well attended, and I was brought up to date on the happenings of extended family members.

In response to questions about my activities, I told them of the busy holiday schedule, followed by the much needed day of rest. I probably convinced them that, unless you enjoyed crowds, Petoskey probably wasn't the best place to be on the fourth of July.

After dinner we played cards around the dining room table. They were surprised to learn that the Reyner family did not play cards, although they did enjoy a variety of table games. We ended our game shortly before eleven, when Dad reminded us that, if we planned to work the next day, we had better get to bed.

Betty and I usually spent a long time talking before going to sleep. That night was no exception. We spoke softly, so as not to wake our younger sisters who were asleep in the next room.

I wanted to hear about her prospective trip to Bermuda. She began by telling me how she and Lorraine had decided that they wanted to go somewhere new and exciting, and after visiting some travel agencies, chose Bermuda.

When I looked at the colored pictures in her brochures, I could see why they had made that choice. It could be an ideal location for a honeymoon, but for Louie and me it would be out of the question. Our funds were invested in our educations.

The following day I returned to work, and the next week enrolled in another summer course called Community Health. I found the subject very informative and relative to my role as teacher.

With work and school the summer passed quickly. I wrote to Louie every day and, as most of my friends had married, spent any remaining time with my family.

Living at home that summer, I became aware of how much my family was changing. I had been one of seven children and accustomed to an active, noisy household. Now all but two remaining at home were adults, and the youthful banter had given way to more serious discussions.

I feared that our close knit family was drifting apart. Our brother Jim had left home shortly after his discharge from the navy, and was living in the south; and our sister Marie was married, living with her husband John and baby daughter outside the city. Betty, Jacqueline, and I would soon go our separate ways; leaving our parents with Joan and Grace, who were almost teenagers. The folks were getting older and showing the signs of aging. I hoped they were up to the challenge!

I didn't have time to dwell on the situation; it was time to hit the books!

Finally it was August, and I was counting the days until Louie's return. School was to begin for both of us on the day after Labor Day, and we had agreed to leave our summer jobs a week earlier to pack, move, and hopefully have some time together.

Louie was right on schedule; and on Friday evening he called to say that he would be arriving in the morning, riding as far as Grand Rapids with his brother Marvin who was to begin work with a publishing company in Stevensville.

They arrived shortly before noon and, after a short visit with my parents and a cup of coffee, Marvin helped Louie move his belongings into the trunk of our car. Then, with a warm farewell and promise to keep in touch, he was on his way.

Soon Mother announced that lunch was ready. While we ate we told the family of our plans for the year ahead.

Dad wondered how we could share a car when we would be so far apart. Louie explained his immediate need to move his belongings to Naperville, "But after that," he said, "I will have no need of a vehicle. The town is small, and I will be living within easy walking distance of the campus. Bev, however, will need transportation to and from school and other educational events, so she will have the car most of the time."

"That's pretty generous of you," Dad replied. "If I can be of any help, just let me know."

That evening Louie and I went to dinner before attending a John Wayne movie at a downtown theater. He stopped at the Y.M.C.A. afterward to inquire about a room for the night, explaining that he didn't want to interfere with a family of girls preparing for church in the morning. He came out of the building with a key, and the promise to "get me to the church on time."

He was true to his word and we left for church the following morning with time to spare, and Joan and Grace in the back seat of the car. Harold Hamilton greeted us as we arrived, and he and Louie stopped to talk as my sisters and I found a place to sit. When Louie joined us he told me about their chat.

"Harold invited us to get together while I am in town," he said; "but I explained that I am only here for the weekend and we have a pretty full schedule. He wondered where I was staying, and when I told him it was at the 'Y', he invited me to stay with them the next time I come to town. I guess their house seems pretty empty since their sons have married and moved away."

After church, we had the traditional Sunday dinner with my family, which included a lengthy conversation around the table. Betty was immersed in her plans for the trip to

Bermuda, and made us all envious as she described the tropical beaches and the lovely hotel where she and Lorraine intended to stay.

By the time we had helped with the dishes and were able to get away, it was the middle of the afternoon. The big meal and lack of exercise left us feeling lethargic. We needed a place where we could walk around and still enjoy some privacy.

John Ball Park was only a little over a mile from our home and was a beautiful place to hike or relax. We left our car in the parking lot while we followed the paths past beautiful ponds and gardens that made the park famous. After an hour or so, we came to a comfortable bench near a pond, where we spent the rest of the day sharing the events of the past six weeks and planning for the days ahead.

Louie would be leaving for Naperville on Tuesday to arrange for housing and take care of business at the college. He planned to return on Friday in time for dinner. He wanted to help me move back to the farm on Saturday; then, according to plan, we would have a couple days together before being separated again for an indeterminate amount of time.

On Monday morning we packed a picnic lunch and headed for Johnson Park, several acres of developed land along the Grand River. There we spent the day, making plans for our future together. When we tired of sitting on a blanket under the tall maple and oak trees, we hiked along the river bank. We didn't dwell on the months of separation that lay ahead, but the years that were to follow when we would be together as man and wife.

We stayed in the park until the sun began to sink in the west; then headed to the nearby town of Grandville. We found a cozy little restaurant on Main Street where we had dinner and lingered over coffee until most of the customers had left and the manager was ready to lock the door. We drove slowly back to Grand Rapids, savoring the time we had together; anticipating another long separation.

Early the next morning Louie left for Naperville and I began packing for my move back to the farm. I filled a large box with books and other material that could supplement my teaching, including the Petoskey stones and small pieces of driftwood from Harbor Springs. I packed my suitcase carefully, mindful of the fall season ahead.

It was late Friday evening when Louie returned. I sympathized with his travel through holiday traffic, especially around Chicago. "Honey," he said, "There is no way I can leave Grand Rapids on Monday morning and arrive back in Naperville before midnight. With the stress of the trip and little sleep, I would be in no shape for my first class, which begins on Tuesday morning at eight.

Finding no alternative, we agreed that he should leave after church on Sunday.

On Saturday morning after breakfast we loaded the car and headed for the Dufort farm. Ellen and Lorraine were at home, waiting for our arrival. We declined the offer of coffee and cookies, in order to begin the task of moving my belongings to my bedroom upstairs. The box of school supplies was heavy, and I appreciated Louie's help. In two trips we had everything moved and more or less settled.

"This is a nice room," he said, looking around, "but you don't have a desk. Where do you correct papers and write letters?"

"At school," I replied. "Julie and Carole Holden will be janitors this year and I can usually finish my work while they are cleaning. I sit on my bed to write letters, read, and complete any unfinished schoolwork. It works for me."

"I was able to rent a room in the home of a nice retired couple in Naperville," he said. "It is smaller than this, but it has a desk, which I really appreciate. You should have one too."

Before leaving I paid Ellen for the first month's rent, which was the same as the year before. We were going out the door when I heard Louie ask her if we might stop back later with another load, and her response, "Of course, any time."

We stopped for hamburgers and malts at a drive-in on Alpine Avenue. As we ate he told me of his trip to Naperville. He had found a room at a price he could afford and within walking distance to the college. He was able to move in and sleep there on Tuesday night and the kind couple even invited him to breakfast on Wednesday morning.

He spent the following day at the college where he was able to confirm his class schedule, establish a tuition plan, and purchase books and supplies.

To his surprise, he found an announcement on the bulletin board advertising for office help in a local furniture company. He called to inquire about the position and, on Thursday afternoon was granted an interview.

The interview went very well and he was given the job, with the provision that work should not interfere with his school schedule.

All in all, he had a very successful trip, for which we were both thankful.

We had left the drive-in and were back on Alpine Avenue when he spotted a furniture store with a sign in the window that read, "Quality Furniture, New or Used." He pulled into the parking lot and we went inside.

A salesman greeted us as we entered, and I was surprised to hear Louie say that he was looking for a desk for his wife; not too big, as it was to be used mainly for writing letters and correcting papers; "she's a schoolteacher," he added.

"I think this is just what you're looking for," the salesman said, pointing to a pretty little walnut desk. "It was made by Widdicomb Furniture Company, right here in Grand Rapids. They make some of the finest furniture in the country!"

We looked it over carefully. Louie was impressed with the tongue in groove construction of the drawers; while I was more interested in the beautiful walnut finish and the two compartments on top that could hold stamps and other small necessities.

"Do you like it?" he asked, with a smile.

"I love it!" I responded.

"Then we will take it," he said to the sales man, "and we'll need a desk lamp to go with it."

The two men carried our purchases to the car, and wrapped the desk carefully in a moving blanket before wedging into the trunk. "You can return the wrap the next time you come this way," the salesman said as he thanked us for the business."

Ellen was surprised when we returned so soon, and more so when she saw what we brought with us. Harry helped Louie carry the desk up to my room, and I followed with the lamp. We took a while to determine the location that would provide the best light for my work. When we finished, Ellen came up to admire our choice. "It's a beautiful desk, and looks just right in here," she said.

We stopped at the furniture store to return the blanket on our way back to Grand Rapids and arrived just in time for dinner. The Saturday night meal in our home was traditionally goulash, and that night was no exception.

After our busy day we were both tired, so decided to just spend the evening with the family and watch The Lawrence

Welk Show on television. Mother made popcorn enough for everyone, and we enjoyed the quiet evening together.

Eventually the rest of the family went to bed, and Louie and I had the living room to ourselves. We hardly spoke, not knowing what to say. He would be leaving the next day, and we did not know when we would see each other again.

Finally I broke the silence with an offer. "Tomorrow, after church, I can take you as far as Benton Harbor. We can have dinner along the way. From there you can get a ride to Naperville and I can drive back home. Then we will both be ready to begin school on Tuesday."

He accepted my suggestion with a little smile; knowing that we were just postponing the inevitable separation.

We had intended to slip out of church right after the benediction, but were stopped by old friends who wanted to talk. Even the pastor detained us with questions about the college and seminary that he had attended several years before.

It was dinner time when we finally left the church, but we decided to travel as far as Holland before stopping to eat. From there the highway led south to Benton Harbor, where Louie would connect with his ride back to Naperville.

It was a somber trip, although we made an effort to think positively. It seemed that we were headed in different directions, hopeful that our love would survive the test of another separation.

# CHAPTER 15

## Changes

The first day of school dawned bright and clear. I woke early, full of enthusiasm, anticipating another year of teaching in my one room country school.

I had returned to the farm the previous afternoon, in time for another delicious meal with the Dufort family. After dinner, instead of socializing or watching television, I excused myself and went up to my room where I spent the evening at my new desk working on lesson plans and writing to Louie. When my work for the night was finished, I fell asleep and dreamt I was back in the classroom with the students of the year before.

The smell of coffee alerted me to the fact that breakfast was ready, and if I wanted to arrive at school before the children, I didn't have time for daydreaming. I finished dressing and, after straightening my room, went downstairs to join Ellen for breakfast. We didn't linger at the table; she knew I was in a hurry to be on my way. As I was leaving, she handed me my lunch and wished me a good day.

No one was at the schoolhouse when I arrived, but someone had certainly been there, for my desk was covered with books and supplies. I set to work unpacking boxes and distributing the contents to their proper places. With the desktop finally cleared, I sat down to rest and catch my breath.

When I casually opened the long desk drawer, I was dismayed to find the attendance sheet and class record book. Transferring information from one document to the other was a time consuming task. If only I had stopped at the school before going to the farm, the room would have been in order, and the names properly transposed from one record to the next. However, there was no time for self recrimination; it was time to get back to work.

It wasn't long before the children began to arrive. Through the open windows I could hear their happy voices as they greeted one another. I glanced at the clock and found that there was enough time to enter a few more names in the class record book before I should ring the bell for school to begin.

I was engrossed in my work, when I looked up to see Jerry Manning come into the building. He was holding his arm and, when I spoke to him, he looked at me with tears in his eyes. Thinking that he might have had an accident on the playground, I became very concerned; but when I asked how he had hurt his arm, he was hesitant to tell me. Finally he responded in a soft voice, "That new kid socked me."

This was an occurrence unheard of the year before. There had been no violence or even verbal abuse at the school during my first year of teaching. I had often considered myself extremely fortunate to have such wonderful students. Now, evidently we had a bully in our midst.

I was preparing to go out to confront this ruffian when Allen Norman and Steven Powell came into the building. They were very upset, having suffered the same treatment as Jerry at the hands of this new kid, whose name, they told me, was Lee Bitely.

I sent the three boys outdoors to tell the culprit that I wanted to see him at my desk right away, and that school would start after this Lee Bitely and I had a talk to set things straight.

I was checking the attendance sheet for the name when a little boy came in and stood in front of my desk. He was so small that all I could see was his curly brown hair, which was wet with sweat, and his big brown eyes. I instructed him to come and stand before me where, from a sitting position, I could look into his face. Before I could say a word, he said, in a solemn voice, "Teacher, them kids been picking on me."

There was no need to identify the protagonist in the conflicts; I had no doubt that Lee Bitely was standing before me looking very guilty and three very reliable witnesses had testified as to his guilt. The question in my mind was who had put him up to it. A five year old does not begin his first day of school ready to fight unless an older person has convinced him of the need to do so.

He stood before me like a prisoner awaiting his sentence. The nice white shirt that was no doubt clean when he left home that morning was now damp and streaked with dirt.

I decided that, under the circumstances, this little boy needed to know the rules before being punished for breaking them. "Lee," I said, in a stern voice, "in this school fighting is not allowed. That means there is no hitting, or kicking, or any other mean behavior. If people have a problem, they come to me and we talk it over. That is how we settle our problems. Do you understand?"

The look of surprise on his face convinced me that this was contrary to what he had been told, but after I asked him the second time, he nodded his head and said, "Yes."

Assured that he would think twice before attacking another schoolmate, I rang the bell and invited the rest of the children inside to begin the new school year.

Five new students joined the school that year; three in kindergarten, one in the fourth grade, and one in the eighth. The other students were making them feel at home by showing them around the building, and explaining our seating arrangement.

After everyone was seated I introduced our new students by name and grade: Ray Dimick was in the eighth grade;

Ellen Ray, in the fourth; and Lee Bitely, Craig Turner, and Linda Powell; in the kindergarten.

Next I explained the daily procedure, beginning with our opening exercises. Then, in accordance with our schedule, we stood for the Pledge of Allegiance to the flag. I was impressed to see the kindergarten children, after watching the others, put their little hands over their hearts and attempt to say the words.

The first assignment was the same for every grade; but instead of a list of things they had done that summer, I asked them to write or draw a picture of the most interesting or exciting event. When finished, they were to study the first lesson in their spelling books. The older children knew just what to do, and went right to work on their assignments, while I met with the new kindergarten class.

Except in size, the three children at the table did not resemble one another in the least. Lee had a sturdy, athletic build, and a tan that indicated a love of the outdoors, while the other little boy was blond, with blue eyes and fair skin. The little girl had dark curls, rosy cheeks, and a smile that was contagious. I was anxious to learn more about each one.

I had already become acquainted with Lee Bitely, but at my invitation he told us more about himself. His daddy worked in Grand Rapids and did a little farming on the side. He had twin brothers who were four years old and would be coming to school next year.

Linda Powell's brother was in the first grade, and her daddy was a dairy farmer. She looked nothing like her red haired brother Steven, who became engrossed in his work when his sister started to speak.

Craig Turner spoke like a little adult as he told us that his father, a chemist, worked in the city and did scientific farming at home.

They had no trouble telling about the exciting things they had done that summer; the problem was limiting them to one event. Finally, after each had selected a favorite, I gave them a sheet of Manila paper and asked them to draw a picture. When they seemed hesitant to begin, I accepted Carole Holden's offer to help them get started while I went on to the next group.

The first graders had grown so much during the summer that they hardly resembled the shy little five year olds who had struggled with the assignment the year before. Their pictures were well underway when I came to their class, and they were ready to tell all about them. As they did so, I wrote a simple sentence for each to copy on the bottom of their paper. Soon they would be able, with a little help, to write their own sentences.

The second and third graders worked independently, occasionally asking for help from the older children when they encountered a difficult word. The fact that kids were allowed to help one another seemed strange to Ray and Ellen who had come from city schools, but they soon understood the advantage of receiving a quick response to a problem when the teacher was busy with another class.

By recess time everyone had finished the morning assignments and was enjoying time on the playground. As I observed their play, I was impressed that no child was left on the sidelines. The older boys and girls were involved in a game that resembled some form of tag; while the younger ones seemed to prefer the playground equipment. Donna Dakins, who had a strong nurturing nature, was helping the younger children at the swings. Age and grade seemed no criteria to the choice of playmates; which I considered a definite advantage of a country school.

Mathematics followed recess and for all but the kindergarten this involved completing the math pretest in the front of their books. From these tests I would be able to determine where each student should begin his math application. Of necessity, math was mostly an individualized study.

The room was quiet while the children were testing, but I heard an occasional snicker as the kindergarteners, for their first math test, were showing me how high they could count. They pronounced the numbers correctly, just not in the right order. With a little practice they would correct their errors. Meanwhile they would concentrate on the numbers one to five.

The daily schedule was the same as the year before. The kindergarten was dismissed at eleven thirty, and the lunch period followed shortly after. In good weather the children ate quickly, anxious to get outdoors for some fresh air and exercise. In bad weather, they lingered over their meal; conversing with their classmates. I enjoyed these lunch periods as they offered an opportunity to observe the children as they related to one another in a relaxed atmosphere.

The afternoon was spent studying the humanities, social studies and science. I tried to enliven the material with spelldowns and some classics that they might find interesting; current events broadened the interest in geography. History posed a problem, but some had traveled or heard stories from parents and grandparents and were willing to share their knowledge with the rest of the students. The children of farmers had learned an astounding amount of science by being around their parents and helping with the chores, and they didn't mind sharing their knowledge with others, including their teacher.

The first book used in the kindergarten was a pre-primer that, by series of pictures, encouraged the children to read from left to right and introduced the characters that they would encounter again in subsequent reading books.

One morning, after they had all become proficient at using the book correctly, I called on Craig Turner to tell a story about the pictures on the page we were studying. "Well," he began in his professorial manner, "in the first picture Blackie is in his yard playing with his ball. Then this little white dog comes to the fence and sees Blackie." Craig paused for a minute or two before continuing, then "Well," he said, "You know, it was the season."

At that the older students burst out in hearty laughter that I could hardly restrain myself, but I gave them a threatening look that meant quiet down and get back to work and, turning my attention to Craig, I asked, "Do you suppose the white dog would like to play with Blackie?"

All three kindergarteners agreed that was probably the case, so we proceeded with the next lesson of the day.

By the middle of the month the school procedures had been adopted and the schedule established, so there was time for some extra-curricular activities. I decided to attempt a "show and tell" period on Friday mornings. The idea received a half-hearted reception from the older students, but the little ones responded enthusiastically.

One Friday morning, Pamela Teesdale asked if she could be first to show and tell that day. She seemed so excited that I couldn't deny her request, so when the time came I announced that Pam had something important to share with all of us. She proudly stepped to the front of the room and, with a happy smile, informed the whole school that her mother was expecting a baby. After my glowing response to Pamela's news, several of the little children stepped forward to say that their mothers were expecting also.

After confirming that there was no pregnancy epidemic in the area, and the session deteriorated into sharing family secrets, I decided that show and tell was not a very good use of time. Most of the children agreed, so it was eliminated completely.

The warm, sunny weather continued throughout the month. The schoolhouse windows were open all day long, and a cool breeze made the classroom comfortable, but the children longed to be outdoors. I sympathized with them and, when their work was done, allowed more time for recess or "physical education."

September slammed the door when she left, with thunder that shook the schoolhouse and lightning that flashed across the darkening sky. The little children cowered on the brink of tears while even the oldest wore worried looks. I provided what comfort I could until the worst of the storm had passed, giving way to a steady rainfall that was quickly turning the playground into a little lake. Then, with an attempt at normalcy, I gathered the kindergarteners around their table for their morning lessons.

I decided to do away with the usual curriculum to talk about the storm that had so upset them. I hoped that as they learned more about the weather, the less threatening it would become. "Does anyone know what causes the rain?" I asked, not expecting an answer.

Craig sat for a minute, with his finger on his forehead, before he responded. "Well," he said in his typical mature manner, "it all begins with vaporation."

With that, Linda jumped up and shouted, "Vaporation! Vaporation!, That's what my daddy has in his milking machine; and that's how it rains, just like a milking machine; squirt, squirt, squirt!"

The whole room erupted in laughter, while Craig, with his hand on his forehead, kept repeating, "No Linda. No Linda. Oh, no Linda!"

I left the kindergarten children with a little book on the rain, too elementary for my budding scientists but the only one on the shelf, to be read by Ruth Holden; while I went on to meet with the first grade.

They had been frightened by the storm also, but quickly regained their composure. We talked about other storms they had experienced in their short lives; then we turned to their daily lessons.

The children worked all day with occasional glances out the window, where the sky had turned a somber grey and the rain continued to pelt the already saturated earth. It was still raining after school when parents came for them.

When I was sure that everyone would get home safely, I picked up my belongings and headed for the farm.

# CHAPTER 16

## Trials and Tranquility

During the night the rain ceased and a cold front moved in from the north. In the morning, as Ellen and I were having breakfast, Harry came in from outdoors. "You will need your coat this morning, Missy; it's pretty cold out there," he warned.

I decided to take his advice and, after breakfast, went to my room to get the jacket that hadn't been worn since the fourth of July. I was in the process of putting it on, when I let out a yelp that made Ellen and Harry come running. My arm felt like it was on fire! As I pulled it out of the sleeve, a family of wasps came with it. Harry and Ellen entered the room and quickly determined the cause of my outburst.

"You go down to the kitchen with Ellen;" Harry said. "She has ingredients in her cupboard that will relieve your pain. Meanwhile, I will deal with the situation up here."

It didn't take long for Ellen to mix up a soothing poultice, which she applied liberally to the wasp stings on my arm. Almost immediately the burning sensation and the swelling began to abate.

I was about to leave for school, when Harry came into the room and handed me my jacket. "Here you are, Beverly," he said. I've checked it over, inside and out, and the wasps are gone. With your permission, I'll be working in your closet today. I need to find the place where the pests entered and seal it so this sort of thing never happens again. We are so sorry it happened to you," he said tenderly.

The change in the weather and the events of my morning led to an impromptu science lesson. The children were curious about the spots on my arm and, after I told of my encounter with the wasps, several of them shared stories of being stung by bees, hornets, and other insects. When I asked why the wasps might have been in my coat sleeve, they hesitated to answer. Finally Jim Long said, "They were looking for a place to get out of the cold."

"That's right," I replied, "and although fall is only beginning, all creatures are preparing for cold weather; even we wore coats or jackets to school this morning. This month let's watch for other animals that are getting ready for winter."

The wind and bright sunlight had cooperated to dry up the mud on the playground and the children were anxious to go outdoors, but the cold wind soon persuaded them to come back inside.

In the days ahead, the weather improved and coats were replaced by sweaters, which were often discarded during some energetic recess activity. The vibrant colors of autumn in Michigan appeared, and we enjoyed what the poets called, "October's bright blue weather.*"

One evening Louie called with an apology and an invitation. He had been looking forward to our weekends together but, because of his work schedule, he was unable to arrange transportation to Michigan with student preachers as we had planned; so, after exploring his options, he decided to pursue another possibility.

"How would you like to come to Naperville next weekend," he asked, "perhaps with your sister Betty, as I wouldn't ask you to make the trip alone? You could visit the campus and look over the town that will soon become our home. We might even be able to take in an event in Chicago."

"I've been looking forward to visiting Naperville," I replied, somewhat hesitantly; "but I was hoping that you and I could make the trip together. Neither Betty nor I have ever been in Chicago, and I understand the traffic is terrible. Also,

---

* Helen Jackson, Poems, Boston: Robert Brothers, 1893

how about accommodations? Are there safe, comfortable motels nearby?"

"There is no need to worry on either count," he said. "You can avoid the Chicago traffic by heading west on Highway 6, south of Chicago. It intersects with Highway 59 which leads north directly into Naperville. It is an easy route, and traffic is usually light, especially in the evening."

"As to accommodations, they are provided free of charge in the women's dormitory as long as you abide by a few simple rules, mainly the weekend midnight curfew."

"I think we can handle that!" I said, with genuine enthusiasm. "I will check with Betty to see if she is available and wants to make the trip."

As soon as he hung up I called Betty to tell her about our invitation. Without hesitation she replied, "That sounds like fun, Bev. I work until five on Friday, but I can be home and ready to leave by five-thirty. If we stop for supper at a fast food restaurant along the way, we can cover quite a distance before dark. The weather is beautiful; it should be a great trip!"

She was always ready for a new venture, and I found her enthusiasm contagious. I went to bed trying to decide what I should pack for a weekend that could include time in the big city of Chicago.

When Betty called the following night I was afraid it was to say that she had changed her mind about making the trip. Instead she asked if we could include another passenger. Evidently, after hearing of our plans, a fellow worker, a girl named Susan, asked if she could ride with us as far as the

Chicago Midway Airport, which was not far from Naperville. She was to meet an uncle and aunt from Wisconsin at the Terminal, and return with them to their home near Green Bay. She agreed to meet our schedule and to help with expenses. I had no problem with accommodating another passenger.

For the rest of the week, I found my thoughts turning to preparations for the weekend. We would probably return late Sunday night, and I would be too tired to plan for the next day of teaching. I decided to alleviate the pressure by remaining at school each afternoon until dinnertime, to correct papers and develop lesson plans for the following week. In the evening I studied the atlas, making sure that the route to Naperville was firm in my mind. By the time I left for home on Friday, I was ready to leave my worries behind and enjoy my brief holiday.

I arrived at my parents house to find Betty and Susan already there and anxious to get on the road. After pausing briefly to greet my parents and listen to some of Dad's wise advice, I joined the other two on the front seat of our little Ford. Soon we were on the highway heading southwest toward Chicago.

Sunset found us at the little town of Union Pier, just north of the Indiana border. We came across a little restaurant that advertised the best hamburgers in the county. I don't know if they won any contests, but they were just what we needed to satisfy our hunger and prepare us for the adventure ahead.

We were back on the highway, talking and laughing as we traveled, when we noticed that the traffic had increased significantly. Expecting to see a sign directing us to Highway 6, we were shocked to see another informing us that we were on Outer Drive heading toward Chicago. When the next sign read "Loop Straight Ahead" I knew that we had to make an exit or we would soon be lost in downtown Chicago.

Since we were now heading north, I decided to turn left at the next road; that should take us west, I determined, in the general direction of Midway Airport.

We continued our journey in near silence; aware that we were in foreign territory. There were few cars on this road, and the dimly lit street signs provided no clue as to our location. We were worried!

Miraculously, the Lord was with us. We first noticed a revolving beacon; next, bright lights; and finally, a plane that was preparing to make a landing. In no time at all we were entering the gates of Midway Airport!

We proceeded to the terminal, where Susan's Uncle and Aunt were waiting. She had accurately described the Ford, and they came to the car before I could find a parking place. They greeted us warmly and thanked us for the safe delivery of their niece. As they unloaded her belongings they gave us directions to Naperville.

We didn't linger to talk, as an attendant was directing us to move and make way for the cars that were arriving to meet the incoming plane; instead we headed back through the gate that led to Highway 50 North.

Betty had become the navigator and was busy studying the map when we came to a rather large city. We evidently appeared bewildered, for while we were stopped at a traffic light, some young men approached the car and asked if they could help us. They were convinced that we were lost for, without our asking, they told us we were in Cicero, not far from Chicago.

When we told them that we were headed for Naperville they confirmed the directions that we had received from Sue's uncle, and added the discouraging fact that we still had a long way to go.

Betty remarked that she was tired and asked if there was a good hotel nearby, and one of the men responded positively, "Just turn right at the next corner, and go for two blocks. It's the red brick building on your right."

We followed his directions and came to a big, dingy structure with one light bulb hanging over the front door. One quick look convinced us; no way would we spend a night in that place! We quickly left the area and resumed our trip north.

Before long we came to Ogden Avenue and turned west toward Naperville. Betty checked her watch and found that it was after eleven; too late to make the weekend curfew at the women's dormitory where we had planned to spend the night. We decided to stop at the next decent appearing motel and go on to Naperville in the morning.

We soon found just what we were looking for. In the pretty little town of Downers Grove was a Holiday Inn with a welcome sign that included the word "VACANCY". While Betty was at the desk registering, I called Louie to assure him of our safety and explain our situation.

He agreed that, under the circumstances, it was best for us to stay where we were, and to meet him for breakfast in the morning at Dinah's Diner, a little restaurant on Main Street in downtown Naperville.

In the morning, refreshed by a good night's sleep, we left the motel and in less than an hour arrived at our destination. We parked the car in front of the eatery, and went inside to find Louie.

Upon entering the restaurant we decided that the food must be exceptionally good, for there was nothing in the appearance of the place to draw the crowd that was already there. Thankfully, Louie had arrived earlier and secured a booth which afforded a modicum of privacy.

Although we were interrupted from time to time by introductions to students whose names we promptly forgot; we succeeded, during breakfast, in sharing the saga of our trip to Naperville.

We left the restaurant well fed and ready for an adventure. First on the agenda was a tour of the area. It was decided that, since he was familiar with the territory, Louie should drive.

When we were comfortably seated and ready to go, he turned the ignition key and . . . nothing happened! He tried again and again; still nothing. "I can't understand it, Bev," he said in disgust. "You can drive this car all over the country without incident; every time I use it, something goes wrong!"

He left us at the car and returned in a short time with a mechanic from the garage down the street. When they looked under the hood, Louie heaved a sigh of relief. "It's just as I thought," said the mechanic, "alternator trouble. It will only take a few minutes to replace it. I'll get to it as soon as I finish with the car I'm working on. Just give me an hour or two. Meanwhile you can leave it right here."

"Well, what would you ladies like to do now that a driving tour is out of the question?"

"Let's just walk around the town," Betty replied. It is a beautiful day, and I had enough riding last night."

I agreed wholeheartedly. "In any case, we can see the town better on a walking tour than from a car," I said.

The rest of our morning was spent exploring "downtown Naperville," which appeared to offer everything that the citizen might need. In addition to stores that sold food and clothing, there were dentists, doctors, lawyers, jewelers, and even shops that sold toys and trinkets to children and visitors like Betty and me. I could imagine, after Louie and I married, browsing through the stores, shopping for gifts for family and friends.

By noon the car was ready and, after paying the mechanic and retrieving the key, we headed for a little ice-cream parlor that was located adjacent to the college campus and on the banks of the Dupage River. For lunch we had a choice of hot dog or hamburger and any of the two dozen flavors of ice-cream on the menu.

The afternoon was spent taking care of business. We registered for a room in the women's dormitory, and deposited our meager belongings. Then we were given a tour of the college itself, everything from the administration building; fondly called "Old Main" to the athletic building and football stadium down by the river.

Louie left us back at the dorm after informing us of the plans for the evening. There was no need to dress for a fancy dinner in Chicago; our travel clothes would be more appropriate for the events that were planned: supper at a local restaurant that offered a chicken dinner for less than a dollar, followed by an evening at the Chicago Sports Arena to see the Ringling Brothers Circus. If time allowed, we would stop for coffee and dessert on the way home. We were glad for time to rest before the evening activities. Surprisingly we found the casual events enjoyable, perhaps more than a fancy dinner in the city.

We didn't foresee the traffic problem we would encounter on our return to Naperville, and as a result arrived at the women's dorm a few minutes after midnight. The door was locked and the dorm mother, who evidently had been roused from her bed, was upset when she finally answered our ring. After Louie, in his usual amiable manner explained the reason for our tardiness, she opened the door wide and told Betty and me to come in quietly and go right to bed.

In the morning we packed our brief belongings before heading to the cafeteria for a breakfast of coffee and cereal. There we met some students who were also visitors to the college; most considering it for future enrollment.

It wasn't long before Louie arrived to take us to church. When we arrived the sanctuary was already crowded, so he invited us to sit in the balcony where the sound and view were superior. The message and music were inspiring and the sanctuary was beautiful, but I missed the fellowship of my home church.

After the service we had dinner at a little restaurant north of town. During the meal we considered when we might next be together. "Thanksgiving is always a big day at our house," said Betty. "Mom goes all out, with turkey, apple and pumpkin pies; the works!"

"Also, there is the big football game that afternoon. It looks like Union will play South High School for the city title."

"It sounds like an occasion I can't afford to miss," Louie responded.

After lunch we drove east on Naperville Road to its intersection with Highway 59. "Just take this road south to Highway 6," he said, "then turn east and you will be headed for home."

When he started to get out of the car, I urged him to allow us to return him to the campus where he was intending to study, for certainly we could find our way from there; but he was determined to walk, saying that he really needed the exercise. So, after a goodbye kiss and a promise to be together again in November, we parted.

Our ride through rural Illinois and Indiana offered little in the way of scenery, so we spent the time talking about our love lives. Betty's fiance' was in the Air Force, stationed in Bermuda: much farther away than Naperville. Although they wrote regularly, she found the separation difficult, but her work and many friends kept her busy and her mind occupied.

I had little time to be lonely. My days were filled with all the requirements of teaching and fellowship with the Dufort family.

Betty was dozing and I was thinking of my students when we crossed the Indiana border into Michigan, where the scenery changed dramatically. Instead of cornfields, we passed woods resplendent in the vivid colors of late October and lakes that rippled in the sun. The effect was invigorating. "If only I could transpose this view into the classroom," I thought, "how stimulating it could be."

I was considering the possibilities, when Betty woke. "If you brought leaves inside, they would die and turn brown in a day;" she said. "You could press them in books between sheets of wax paper or cover leaves with typing paper and color the paper with the flat sides of crayons." Her suggestions were helpful, and I determined to implement them when I returned to the classroom.

We arrived back in Grand Rapids in time to enjoy a late supper with our family. After a short visit, I called Louie to tell him that we had arrived safely. As it was still early, I decided to return to the farm; leaving Betty to give her rendition of our trip to the family.

The sun was setting in the west as I drove north to Algoma Township. The beautiful red and gold gradually turned to shades of purple and, by the time I left the highway, it was dark.

It reminded me of the changing seasons, and how little time remained to enjoy the brilliant colors of autumn. "So it is with life;" I thought. "Before long I would be leaving my wonderful country school for a new life in the suburbs of Chicago;" The thought left me ambivalent, feeling both joy and sorrow.

By the time I arrived at the farm it was getting late and I was very tired. I provided the Dufort family with a brief summary of our trip to Naperville before excusing myself and heading for bed. I was glad that I had taken the time to prepare lesson plans in advance.

The following morning, as I drove to school, I decided to revise those plans to include the appreciation of the beautiful world around us. During our opening exercises I told the children of the sunset, the colored leaves, and the lakes that I had seen on my trip. "Tomorrow let's bring some of that beauty inside and try to make it last a little longer. Pick the prettiest leaves you can find and bring them to school. We will find a way to preserve them and use them to decorate the room." To end the discussion, I read a portion from Psalm 19, beginning with the words "The heavens declare the glory of God; and the firmament proclaims His handiwork . . ."

The following day the children returned to school with their hands full of brilliantly colored leaves. We briefly discussed the scientific process by which sunlight caused chemicals in the trees to produce chlorophyll causing the leaves to turn green; and as the light diminished, produced the beautiful colors of autumn; until finally the leaves fell to the ground and turned brown.

Now we were going to try to keep the leaves colorful for a while longer. I suggested the methods Betty and I had discussed, but allowed the students to choose a technique that they might enjoy. However, their lessons were to be their first priority.

After their reading lesson, I helped the kindergarten get started with their art project. They seemed bored with the big crayons that they used almost daily, so I decided to introduce them to a new medium.

In the storage room I found Prang Paints: watercolors in black metal boxes. Along with them were brushes, little paper cups, and the appropriate paper for painting. After the three were seated at their table with the utensils in front of them, I showed them how to dip the tip of the brush in water and then in the paint to make beautiful autumn colors.

I had left the kindergarteners to their task and was working with the first grade, when I felt a gentle tap on my shoulder. I turned to see Craig Turner standing beside me, looking very distressed. "Teacher," he complained, "Lee Bitely painted me."

I stopped what I was doing and returned to the kindergarten table to deal with the problem. Lee's first response was a denial, followed by an accusation. "You painted me first," he declared.

"Why would I do a silly thing like that?" Craig Responded.

I interrupted the argument by declaring firmly that the only place for the paint was the paper in front of them. As I left I glanced at little Linda. She was busy working on her work of art, totally ignoring the boys at the table with her.

It wasn't long before Craig returned with the complaint that Lee was at it again, and had painted the sleeve of his new sweater. I returned to the seat of the crime, and this time threatened to take the paints away, for evidently Lee wasn't ready to use them correctly. This time he didn't deny touching Craig's sleeve with his paint brush, but pointed out that it didn't leave a mark.

When Craig came back a third time, I ran out of patience! I ordered Lee to pick up his chair and head for the cloakroom where he was to remain until recess time when the two of us would have a talk.

The room was unusually quiet for the rest of the morning, as the children had never before seen their teacher angry. They evidently didn't suffer from the experience however, for later I discovered that they had produced some exceptional artwork.

It was time for recess and, as was their habit, several of the students went to the cloakroom for midmorning snacks. A few returned a few minutes later to report, disgustedly, that their desserts were missing from their lunchboxes.

I called Lee back into the classroom determined to deal severely with this problem child, but first I wanted to hear what he had to say. There was no doubt that he had helped himself to those goodies knowing that they belonged to someone else, so I began by asking, "Why did you take those desserts, Lee, when you knew that was stealing?"

"I was so hungry," he replied.

In response to my questioning, he told me his story. With tears running down his cheeks, he said, "We didn't have any breakfast this morning, because my daddy is in the hospital with a broken leg."

By now he was sobbing, so I put my arm around him as he continued: "You see, our cow got out last night and my daddy was chasing her."

At that point he had experienced my full sympathy, which dissipated as the story progressed: "Then the cow climbed a tree, and my daddy pulled her tail to get her down. The cow fell on my daddy and broke his leg."

He was still crying when he finished his story, and I was amazed that a five year old could concoct such a story and become so emotionally involved in its narration. "Take your chair and go to the corner near your table, and think about the story you just told me," was the only punishment I could give him.

I don't know what the rest of the children thought when they came inside and found that he had been crying, but they were quite subdued for the rest of the day.

October ended with one of the children's favorite events: the annual Halloween party. The rains came, the wind blew, and the leaves covered the ground. While the faint of heart remained in the schoolhouse playing games and bobbing for apples, heartier souls donned winter coats for the hay ride which had become an integral part of the occasion. I guess I had survived my indoctrination the year before as I didn't spend much time running behind the wagon on this, my second excursion. The party, as usual, was a big success; in part because it was a warm friendly place to spend a cold October night.

# CHAPTER 17

## Holiday Surprises

The grey November days didn't dampen the enthusiasm of the children inside the Gougeburg School. The holiday season was approaching! The stores were brightly decorated and the media was counting down the shopping days until Christmas.

Thanksgiving Day, with its historical and religious significance, was often overshadowed by the more popular holiday. I didn't want that to be the case in our school. I planned my lessons for the month to include information about life in early America, including American Indians as well as white settlers.

Rather than attempting another movie after the fiasco of the year before, I resorted to the written word and pictures for most of our data. From the tepee I had purchased in Petoskey and pictures of hogans, the children could envision the environment of the Native Americans that had once lived in our area.

Of course, the season wouldn't be complete without stories of the Pilgrims and reference to turkeys and pumpkin pie. The little children enjoyed making costumes and Indian headdresses from brown paper bags and drawing around their hands to make turkeys, while some of the older ones made place cards to adorn their holiday tables. Some activities had become traditional.

One activity, which wasn't really associated with the Thanksgiving season, but often occurred simultaneously, was the construction of paper snowflakes to decorate the windows. This occurred on the day of the first snowfall, when the children were too excited to keep their minds on their lessons and could hardly wait to get out the door to play in the cold, white stuff.

The days passed quickly, and it was soon time for the holiday weekend. On Wednesday, after the children had left, Mr. Teesdale arrived bringing my paycheck and the message I had been expecting.

"Folks really enjoyed the kids Christmas program last year, and are looking forward to another next month," he said. "Can we count on you to prepare a presentation for the evening of December twenty-third, before the Christmas holidays begin?"

He seemed relieved when I answered in the affirmative and he offered additional words of encouragement: "The men will be here to set up the stage this weekend, and Mrs. Huizenga has agreed to accompany the children on the piano, as she did last year." I thanked him for his help and wished him a happy Thanksgiving.

After he left I gathered up my belongings and headed for Grand Rapids and my reunion with my family and fiance'. On the way, I stopped at the farm to wish my surrogate family a happy holiday.

As I approached the city, my thoughts turned to the weekend ahead. I was able to put aside any concerns I might have had for Christmas activities at the school; for this year I knew what to expect and had given forethought and some preparation for the ensuing events. Now I could relax and enjoy the Thanksgiving holiday.

It was dinner time when I arrived home, but the delicious smells emanating from the kitchen were not for the evening fare. "We are just having goulash and canned fruit tonight," Mother said. "The food on the kitchen table is for our dinner tomorrow." We enjoyed a simple but ample meal, embellished by engaging conversation and the pleasure of being together again.

Shortly after dinner, while I was helping my sisters with the dishes, Louie arrived. He had received a ride to the city with a seminary student, and from his church took a short bus ride to our home. He declined Mother's offer of goulash, saying that they had stopped for hamburgers at a little town along the highway.

As we were finishing our kitchen chores, he asked if I was interested in going to the community Thanksgiving service which was being held at our church that year. I responded enthusiastically and thought of asking others to join us, but from the look on his face I could discern that Louie would rather we go alone.

Hope Church was a special place for us, not only as a place of worship but it was there we first met and developed a friendship that had blossomed into love and would soon culminate in marriage. We held hands as the minister reminded us all of how much we had for which to be thankful. I counted my blessings as I thought of Louie's safe return from the service, the love of family and friends, and the special children in my little country school.

After the service we went to a little restaurant not far from my home that was well known for excellent desserts. We lingered over hot fudge sundaes and coffee, completing our plans for the weekend and talking about the future, until the manager dimmed the lights and started to lock the door.

We both enjoyed football, and Thanksgiving was the day for the traditional high school confrontation between my alma mater, Union, and our archrival from across town, South High School. This year, as was often the case, they were competing for the city championship. We decided to go to the game, even if it resulted in our being late for dinner.

We arrived at my home to find the house dark, except for a little night light that came from the kitchen. Evidently the family had retired early in preparation for the busy day ahead. We said goodnight on the front porch and agreed to meet the next morning in time to be at the football stadium well before the noon-time kickoff.

Louie had arrived and we were about ready to leave for the game, when Dad issued a warning. "It's cold out there, and according to the morning paper it will be getting colder. Be sure to wear something warm; that jacket may be too thin for this weather."

I went to the closet and retrieved an old navy p-coat that my brother had left when he moved south. It was big, but with a sweater underneath it served the purpose. Louie was wearing a leather jacket with a fake fur collar that he could pull up around his ears. I added a scarf and mittens to my ensemble and thought we were ready for whatever Mother Nature could deliver, when my mother came into the room carrying an old woolen army blanket. "You might want something to sit on," she said.

As the game got under way the crowd on the bleachers, along with our blanket and warm clothing, provided the protection we needed from the cold wind which was blowing across the field; but as time passed, the temperature dropped and people began to leave the stadium. At half-time snow flurries accompanied the marching band members, and by the end of the third quarter the entire field was covered with snow, obliterating the yardage lines. Still the diehard fans remained and the game went on.

By the fourth quarter, the weather had become a virtual blizzard, and we watched the dark shadows of the players as they dashed across the field through the cloud of white. With the blanket now over our heads and wrapped around us, we remained to see our team successfully kick the field goal that won the game and made them the city football champions.

We arrived home, cold and wet, but exhilarated by the excitement of the game. After removing our damp outerwear, we joined the family who were already seated around the heavily laden Thanksgiving table. After a silent Grace, we enjoyed a delicious turkey dinner with all the trimmings, followed by a slice of Mother's mouth-watering apple pie.

We spent the rest of the day and the next visiting with family and friends, but on Saturday Louie surprised me with a mysterious invitation. "Let's go for a ride," he said. "There is something I want you to see." I was full of questions, but he would share no clue as to our destination.

We drove through the city and headed south on Division Avenue toward the suburbs. I was surprised when he pulled into the lot of a used car dealership. While we sat in the car and the salesmen waited on other people, Louie shared what was on his mind.

"The Ford has been a good little car for you," he began; "but every time I use it, there is a problem. Also, it doesn't perform very well in cold weather. As I recall, last winter Bob and Harry had to pull it around the driveway with a tractor just to get it started. What would you do if it stalled when you were alone somewhere?"

He had finished making his case when the automobile salesman approached, and with a happy smile said," Is there something I can help you with today?"

"We are considering the purchase of another car," Louie replied, "and a friend of mine, Charlie Carter, recommended your dealership. We have only started to look around."

"Well, come into my office where it's warm, and we will see if we have anything that might suit your needs. By the way, my name is Andy Truman, no relation to the president, I'm sorry to say."

We entered a small but neat office where, after we were seated around his desk, he pulled out a rather thick file and began ruffling through the pages. "Now, what exactly are you looking for in a car?" he asked.

Louie proceeded to tell him about our circumstances, stressing our need, above all, for a safe, dependable vehicle. "A clean, attractive car with low mileage would be preferred," he said, "but our available cash is limited."

"There is a car on the lot that would suit your needs," Andy replied, "but I hesitate to show it to young people like you. It's an old person's car, a light grey Oldsmobile Ninety-Eight that was owned by a local banker who traded cars every other year. It is in excellent condition and clean as a whistle. Why don't you take it for a little ride while I make a few calls to see what I can do about the financing.

We drove through the suburbs and out onto the highway to test the car at various speeds. Then Louie turned onto an unpaved country road and invited me to take the wheel. "This is the type of road you travel regularly," he said. "Let's see how the car handles under these conditions."

The ride was amazingly smooth, with the car automatically adjusting to the irregular terrain. Finally, there was nothing about the car to dissuade us from buying it, except, probably, the price.

While we were away, Andy had been busy dealing with that concern. He was fairly certain that once we drove the car we would want to buy it. After determining the Blue Book price, and checking with the local bank, he came up with a price and payment schedule that we could accept.

After signing the necessary papers and receiving two sets of keys, we drove to the bank where we completed the transaction and left with a coupon book that entitled us to make monthly payments over a period of two years. "If we both work this summer, we can have the car paid for before the due date," Louie said optimistically.

We returned home that afternoon, surprising the family with our new purchase. After they had checked it over thoroughly, Louie provided short rides for a few at a time around the area.

While he was away I had a talk with Dad who, I could tell from his stern demeanor, thought that we had gone out on a limb in buying such an expensive automobile. After

I told him the price and explained our payment plan, he relaxed and smiled as he said, "It's a beautiful car, and I hope it makes you both very happy; but if you ever have trouble making those payments, don't hesitate to come to me."

The following morning we surprised our friends at church by driving up in our big new car. They checked it over thoroughly, before remarking jokingly that it could handle a good-sized family. "Or a bunch of school kids," Louie replied.

After dinner, we drove across town to the church where Louie was to meet his friend for the ride back to Naperville. While we rode, he asked, "Now that you have had time to think it over, Honey, did we do the right thing in buying this car?"

"I had my doubts at first," I admitted, "but you presented a sound rationale, and now I think we made the right choice. I must admit that I miss my little Ford. It was my first car and took me on many happy adventures; but it was getting old and probably unsafe; so I am glad we made the change."

We met Charlie at the church, and the first thing he did was admire our new wheels. "Thanks for recommending your friend Andy," Louie said. "He was a gentleman and I think he gave us a good price on this car."

"Oh, by the way," he said, almost as an afterthought; "this is my fiancée, Beverly Haskins, the joint-owner of the car." We laughed about how I rated in the scheme of things.

The men loaded Louie's belongings into Charlie's car, and soon they were on their way back to Naperville, where they would remain until their Christmas break.

I went back home to pack my few belongings before heading to the farm. They looked so small in the huge trunk of the Oldsmobile that I decided to move everything to the back seat. Once settled, I went inside to thank my parents for a wonderful weekend and bid my sisters goodbye.

It was nearly dark when I arrived at the farm, and the family was in the living room watching television when they noticed a strange car turning into the driveway.

Harry went to the back door and turned on the yard light. He was astounded when I got out of the big, grey vehicle, and greeted him with, "Hi Harry. How do you like our new car?"

"Stay right there," he ordered; then turned back inside. "Ellen, Lorraine. Bob," he shouted, "Come out here. Bev is here and she has something to show us."

They looked the car over carefully, from engine to tail lights. Finally Lorraine said, "It looks like a very nice car; but I'm freezing. Let's go inside where it's warm."

I parked the car, grabbed my belongings, and joined the others in the living room. They didn't ask, but I explained how Louie and I had made the decision to buy another car, and why we chose a big Oldsmobile sedan.

"I think you and Louie made the right decision," said Harry. "You don't know how we worried about you whenever you headed up north in that little Ford."

The others nodded in agreement and as I headed for my room I felt a sense of belonging to the Dufort Family.

The following morning I parked the new car in my usual parking space and waited for the reaction of the children as they arrived for school. I was surprised when the door opened slowly, and Donald Manning peeked into the room. "It's Miss Haskins," he shouted to the others who were milling around outside.

They came bounding into the room full of questions. They evidently thought the car in front of the school belonged to a substitute teacher, and hesitated to come inside until they had checked her out. After I explained my need for another, more dependable car, they settled down for the work of the day.

During our regular morning exercises, I offered a pep talk that I hoped would energize the class for the busy month ahead. "Our Christmas vacation will begin in three short weeks," I said, "and we have a lot to accomplish before then."

I stepped onto the stage and asked, "Does everyone know why this platform is in the room?"

"For our Christmas program," replied Carole Holden.

"That's right," I replied. "Most of you were in the program last year, and you know how much time it takes to prepare. Mrs. Huizenga, the wife of the Baptist minister, has agreed to accompany us on the piano again, but those of you who have speaking parts may have to work on them at home."

"Now," I continued, "What else do we do in December in addition to our regular studies?"

The answers came from everywhere: "Decorate the room, make Christmas cards, presents for our parents; and how about a Christmas tree?" Earl Manning added.

"I expect a Christmas tree will arrive in a day or two. Meanwhile, it sounds like we have plenty to do. Are we up to it?" I queried.

They responded enthusiastically and immediately set to work. A variety of art supplies were on the bookshelf at the back of the room, as were copies of the "Grade Teacher" which was filled with ideas for Christmas projects.

The Kindergarteners appeared a little bewildered by all the activity, so I decided to begin their class talking about familiar things, like how they spent Thanksgiving. When they each had shared their story, we turned to their regular lessons.

All three were already reading fluently, and seemed to enjoy the process. Their math lesson that day would conclude with an art project: they would use the green and red strips of construction paper to practice counting, adding, and subtracting, before making them into paper chains.

As I went around the room from class to class, I found most students had completed their assignments and were already working on Christmas projects. I checked their work carefully, afraid some might have carelessly rushed through their lessons to spend time on more enjoyable activities; but that was usually not the case.

The days flew by. The kindergarten chain went all around the room. The Christmas tree had arrived and was standing next to the stage, beautifully decorated in a variety of donated ornaments and student creations. The program had been rehearsed over and over, until I was sure every child knew his or her part. In short, we were ready for Christmas; or so I thought.

It was the evening of the big event. I dressed in my holiday outfit and headed for the schoolhouse right after dinner. I arrived to find the building unlocked and people busily setting extra chairs in the aisles and along the back of the room. "It looks like we are expecting a crowd," I said to a man who was unloading chairs from a pickup truck.

"That's usually the case," he replied. "The school Christmas program is one of the big social events of the season. Shucks, folks who don't have any kids or grandkids come just to see the show. It's always entertaining; you never know what to expect."

"By the way, I'm Ted Jenkins," he said, as he offered his hand.

"And I'm Beverly Haskins, the teacher" I replied

The building filled quickly, and I was led to believe that Mr. Jenkins was right. I was glad that I had reserved the little chairs in the front row for my younger students; the older ones were seated on folding chairs along the back of the stage.

At seven o'clock Mr. Teesdale took the stage and the room became amazingly quiet. He introduced me with some kind words that needed no response; and I, in turn, introduced Linda Powell, who would be giving the welcome.

She looked adorable, dressed in a pretty red Christmas dress, as she confidently made her way to the middle of the stage. I knew that she would do a good job because she had delivered her speech perfectly just that morning; so I was shocked when, after giving the crowd a big smile, she said in a loud voice, "What are you all looking at me for? I ain't gonna say nothing."

I was embarrassed, more for myself than for her, for she seemed completely nonchalant; but the crowd laughed heartily, and seemed to thoroughly enjoy her mischief.

The program progressed smoothly until it came time for the second grade boys to give their performance. They were to recite a poem by Marchette Chute, entitled "Christmas Mittens," with each boy taking a stanza. They knew their parts perfectly, and I was sure that they would recite the humorous poem without a problem; but I had overlooked one complication: earlier in the week Stephen Powell had lost his two front teeth. As a result, the poem became even more humorous.

The boys looked very serious as they lined up across the front of the stage, each carrying a pair of mittens. They recited their parts in sequence:

Allen Norman:      I wanted a rifle for Christmas,

                     I wanted a bat and a ball,

                     I wanted some skates and a bicycle,

                     But I didn't want mittens at all.

Wayne Wainwright:  I wanted a whistle and I wanted a kite,

                     I wanted a pocketknife that shut up tight,

                     I wanted some boots and I wanted a kit,

                     But I didn't want mittens one little bit.

Steven Powell:       I told them I didn't want mittenth;

                     I told them ath plain ath plain,

                     I told them I didn't want mittenth,

                     But they've given me mittenth again.

When the audience started to laugh Steven looked confused, and I thought he might start to cry, but their enthusiastic response and warm smiles evoked a toothless grin instead.

The second part of the program involved most of the older kids. I felt that it wouldn't be a Christmas program without commemorating the source of our celebration: so we decided to include a portrayal of the Nativity.

Of course, Julie Holden and Ray Dimmick, the eighth graders, played Mary and Joseph; and the rest of the cast: angels, shepherds, and wise men; was filled by volunteers from the upper grades. Linda Dakens presented a moving rendition of the poem "If Bethlehem Were Here Today", and Christine Long closed the pageant with a beautiful solo of everyone's favorite, "Silent Night."[2]

Last, but certainly not least, was Santa Claus; who arrived right on cue to the singing of "Jingle Bells."

I mingled with the crowd for a while, before accepting my check and a rather generous Christmas gift, and heading for my own celebration of the holiday.

The Christmas program was still on my mind as I traveled the familiar road back to Grand Rapid. I smiled as I recalled Linda's Powell's surprise announcement, Steven's missing teeth, and the beautiful pageant with the special enhancement of Linda's poem and Christy's solo. The children never ceased to surprise me with their hidden talents. I couldn't entertain the thought of leaving them and moving on with my life; at least at that time.

However, shortly after arriving home, I received a call from Louie and my anticipation of the future returned. He was on his way to Grand Rapids, and planned to stay with his friend from the Seminary that night. "But tomorrow is Christmas Eve," he said, "and I would like to do something

---

[2] Roberts, Elizabeth Madox. "Christmas Morning." Stories, Poems & Humor, Printable 11 Apr. 2013 Web : Santa Search.Org

special, just the two of us. Do you suppose we could celebrate with your family later?" I assured him that they were adaptable, and probably my sister Jackie would be with her fiance' and his family that night.

When I asked about his plans for the evening all he said was, "There is this little German restaurant called the Schnitzelbank where we can have dinner, and a Doris Day movie is showing at the theatre nearby. I never know what to give you for Christmas and I thought you might enjoy a "night on the town."

"That sounds wonderful," I replied, and immediately began planning for the special event ahead. My family was willing to postpone our traditional celebration until Christmas day when the whole family could be together, and Betty offered to help me get ready for my big date.

I spent a good share of the next day preparing for the evening events. My sister's were very helpful with their opinions of my dress and hairstyle, assisting me whenever they could. Finally, looking my best and wearing some of Betty's expensive perfume, I was ready for Louie when he arrived at five o'clock.

The evening was delightful: the ambiance and food at the restaurant was superb, and the movie had us laughing at the antics of Doris Day. As we left the theatre I squeezed his arm and thanked Louie for the wonderful Christmas gift.

` To my surprise, he smiled and replied, "The night isn't over yet."

We returned to the car, and drove around town until we came to Lookout Park: the highest point in the city which overlooked the downtown area and the river beyond. There Louie parked the car and from the glove compartment withdrew a beautifully wrapped little box. With his arm around me he said, "I've been waiting to give this to you for a long time, but with my income it has taken a while to get exactly what I wanted. I made the final payment last week, and now it is all yours, because I love you, Beverly."

I didn't know whether to laugh or cry, but I guess I did a little of both as I opened the little velvet box that contained a gleaming diamond solitaire: my engagement ring.

We stayed in the park until nearly midnight, talking about the future and making plans for our wedding. Finally we decided that the wonderful evening must come to an end, for tomorrow was Christmas, another special day.

We parted on our front porch, as I expected everyone to be in bed; but to my surprise I found Betty still awake and waiting for my return. I showed her my ring and was telling her about our evening, when Jackie came into the room. Holding out her left hand, she displayed her bright, shining engagement ring. Betty had received her ring sometime earlier; so we sat together comparing our rings and discussing our wedding plans until early the next morning.

The next day the family gathered for a big Christmas dinner and the sharing of gifts all around. Stories were told of past Christmases when as children we rose before dawn to see if Santa had arrived. After sending us back to bed a time or two, our parents relented and let us open our presents and help ourselves to some of the goodies on the dining room table. Later, we would go to our grandparent's farm for Christmas dinner, more presents, and even an impromptu rendition of Dickens Christmas Carol.

In the evening we were all invited to the home of our uncle Russ and aunt Ann in the little town of Nunica. There Louie was welcomed into the extended Haskins family. We ended the day around the piano, singing our favorite Christmas carols while our uncle Don played.

As Louie and I parted that night we agreed that it was the most wonderful Christmas of our lives.

# CHAPTER 18

## Mission Completed

The holiday season was over and the children had returned to school, enthusiastic and happy to be back with their friends. They greeted me warmly and were telling me about their Christmas activities and gifts, when someone noticed the diamond ring on my finger.

"Yes, it is an engagement ring, and I received it from my fiance' Louis on Christmas Eve," I responded to the questions that were coming to me from all directions. "During our opening exercises I want to hear about the special gifts you received; but for now please take your seats so I can make sure that everyone is here."

After the Pledge of Allegiance, "God Bless America," and a Scripture reading; the children took turns sharing some of the joys of the Christmas holidays. After everyone had been given a chance to speak, we turned to the business at hand: schoolwork.

Most teachers will agree that the winter months are the most productive teaching periods of the year. Uninterrupted by holidays and most outdoor activities, it is possible to concentrate on the curriculum and identify the weak areas and the students who need extra help. I found that to be the case.

The weather was not conducive to outdoor activities, so the students spent recess periods playing games or just visiting. It might have been a boring time, except for their creativity. They found ways to amuse themselves with whatever resources were available.

Early in February they began preparing for Valentine's Day. After their lessons were finished, they spent time making lists and creating cards and paper hearts to decorate the room. The older children created a mailbox and chose a postman to deliver the mail during the little party that was held to commemorate the day. Long after the celebration was over the festive artwork decorated the room.

March arrived with a fluctuation of weather that belied the advent of spring. A cold rainy day might be followed by snow flurries or an occasional interval of sun. The playground remained too muddy for any outdoor activity. The children, primarily the young ones, were tired of being confined to the room. My promise that spring was on its way fell on deaf ears. I decided that something must be done to inspire them.

One day, when the weather allowed, I took the kindergarten children out to the playground where, with a big spoon, we filled a blue enameled basin with mud. After returning inside I invited them to roll up their sleeves and run their fingers through the dirt and tell me if they found anything else in the pan. "Just mud," was their response.

After further examination, they were convinced that it was a basin full of mud that we placed on the window sill; but they agreed to take turns watering it and watch for any change that might occur.

A week or two went by with no change; then one morning Craig Turner, who had the watering assignment that day, exclaimed in amazement, "Teacher, the mud has germinated."

I was as surprised by his terminology as Craig was by the little green shoots that appeared in the black dirt. Other children came to examine the miracle in the basin, and I was afforded an opportunity to teach a science lesson and demonstrate that spring was just around the corner.

It finally arrived: little green leaves replaced the buds on the trees, the songbirds returned, and the children were once again enjoying recess on the playground.

Mother's Day was just around the corner and the children decided, with my prompting, to do something special for their mothers that year: a Mother's Day Tea.

I had read in "The Grade Teacher" that a teacher should invite her superintendent to visit her classroom at least once a year, and decided that was the time to do so. I called the Kent County office of Dr. Clark, and was surprised and pleased when his secretary reported that he would be delighted to come.

For the next two weeks we practiced a little program that the children would perform for the occasion. They chose some of their favorite songs to sing, and Mrs. Huizenga graciously agreed to accompany them on the piano. Some of the older children recited poems or read tributes to mothers. To prevent a serious accident, punch was served instead of tea.

Everything was going well until the youngest children were to demonstrate their knowledge of right and left by singing a little song and extending the appropriate appendages. I was mortified when they sang of their right foot, but extended their left, and when they sang of their left hand, put out the right; for I was certain that they knew better. Mr. Clark just laughed at the faux pas, and the children redeemed themselves by singing the next song faultlessly. Later I realized that I was the cause of their blunder; for I was sitting directly in front of them, providing a mirror image with my prompting.

The rest of the production proceeded without a problem and the mothers seemed to enjoy the program and the cards that the children presented to them at conclusion of the event.

The next few weeks went by quickly. The older children had all passed the Iowa Achievement Test and finished the work in their textbooks, while the youngest were reading and performing simple math functions. Each student demonstrated significant progress over the year before, and everyone was ready for a promotion to the next higher grade.

I accompanied Julie on the eighth grade trip, and became the counselor for a group of girls from many schools. Julie had no trouble blending with the group; she appeared to be already acquainted with many of them. They all seemed to enjoy themselves; especially the final dinner when they were to sit with kids from other schools: boys and girls. I watched as they prepared for the event by continuously combing their hair and, after trying a variety of styles, deciding the original best suited them. They did make one change in their attire. THEY CHANGED THEIR SOCKS!

The following week Ray, Julie and I rode together to the graduation ceremonies held in the auditorium of the Edgerton School, the largest building in the Algoma District. I felt as proud as a parent when they walked across the stage to receive their diplomas. I felt a tenderness too, as they would be moving on; she, to Rockford High School and he, back to his home in Indiana.

The whole class celebrated the last day of school with a little party and I was surprised when Della Holden presented me with a gift from my students, a silver creamer and sugar bowl on a little silver tray.

The children left the building in a joyful mood, no doubt enjoying their freedom and anticipating the carefree summer days ahead. A few looked back and with a wave and a wistful smile. It was then I realized how much I would miss those boys and girls and to what extent they had become a part of my life.

I hadn't given much thought to leaving Gougeburg that spring. I had been too busy planning for my summer wedding. My wedding gown and the dresses for my attendants had to be selected and altered, and Della Holden was working on a dress for Louie's little niece, who was to be our flower girl. With invitations, flowers, and plans for a reception, there was no time for nostalgia.

However that day, after everyone was gone, I sat in my car outside the school house remembering the last two years and the many ways this teaching experience had blessed my life.

I had learned so much from the children: not only that there is a difference between a cow and a steer; but that children, in their innocence can offer wisdom and insight that we as adults are often too self-absorbed to discern. I learned, when shown respect, children will respond in kind; and when they are loved they will try their best to be what you want them to be. I also found that children can learn more from other children than from their teacher.

I left my little country school to marry and accept a position as a third grade teacher in a suburban Chicago elementary school with over a thousand students. Even in that totally different environment I was able to apply the lessons I had learned from the wonderful children in my ONE ROOM COUNTRY SCHOOL.

# CHAPTER 19

## Farewell To The Farm

The road from the schoolhouse to the farm seemed different somehow. The woods that had just recently been garbed in the light pastels of spring were sporting the solemn green of summer. The cattle, back on their knoll, showed no tendency to move from the comfortable shade of an old apple tree. The gravel road was hot and dusty from the recent dry spell. I drove slowly, knowing that I would not travel this route again.

My somber mood improved when I reached the farm. Ellen was in the driveway, surrounded by a flock of chickens. She had been watering her garden and the birds were enjoying whatever the wet ground was producing. I smiled, recalling another time when I met her in the driveway surrounded by hens. That time the biddies were drunk!

I parked the car in my usual space and joined her in the garden where she was shooing the chickens away from her tender vegetable plants. She laughed as we recalled the time in the fall when Bob and Harry had been preparing the silo for winter fodder. The chickens had found the fermented residue from the discarded silage quite tasty, and ate heartily. Ellen's attempt to hose the material from the driveway only added to the problem. I had arrived home in time to see the inebriated fowl teetering around, some on one leg, others crowing like roosters.

"These chickens are perfectly sober," she said, as she acknowledged the hens that were finally vacating her garden and heading toward the henhouse. "They have plenty of food and water in their own enclosure but they prefer my garden and unless the gate is closed securely they head right this way; but let's go inside where it's cooler. I have some fresh lemonade in the refrigerator, and some cookies that I made this morning."

On the kitchen counter, in addition to the cookies, were dinner rolls and a fresh apple pie. "Ellen, you should not be baking on a day like this!" I scolded. "It must be near ninety degrees out there."

She laughed and replied, "I was up at dawn, and finished my baking before Harry and Bob were back from the barn. I had a little trouble keeping them away from the pie, until I reminded them that it was for a special meal, our last dinner with you."

I felt tears welling in my eyes and my cookie was sticking in my throat. I washed it down with a big drink of lemonade and thanked her for the refreshments before heading upstairs to begin packing for my move back to Grand Rapids.

I was removing my clothes from the closet when I noticed the molding that sealed the joint where the wall joined the ceiling below the eave. Harry had had evidently made the repair after my misadventure with the wasps and I never noticed or thanked him. I was recalling the many ways this family had gone out of the way to accommodate me, expecting nothing in return; when Ellen called to invite me to dinner.

The mood around the table that evening was made light as we recalled my first visit to the Dufort farm. Evidently I had impressed Harry and Bob as a poor little kid in need of a home; and they were sure that tender-hearted Ellen would agree to provide one.

Lorraine admitted that she was not keen on inviting a stranger into their home, especially the local schoolteacher. However, as time passed, she accepted me and we eventually became close friends. She even agreed to act as a bridesmaid in my wedding.

Our conversation was interrupted by the sound of an approaching truck that evidently had a bad muffler and a very loud radio. "Is that Herb Conklin taking his poor cow for a walk again?" Ellen asked.

"No, Harry replied. "Herb retired after Christmas and has mended his fences, so Bessie stays at home these days."

We all laughed as we recalled the evening about a year before when we had been at the same table enjoying another of Ellen's delicious meals. Through the open windows we heard the sound of an approaching truck and a loud voice shouting, "So you want to go for a walk, do you? Well, I'll take you for a walk."

We had watched as an old farmer drove past the house. He was leaning out of the truck window, shouting at his cow that was tied to the back of the vehicle by a long rope. The cow was bellowing her reply which might have been interpreted, "So you want some milk tonight, do you?"

"I have really enjoyed life on the farm," I said as I looked around the table at the people who had become a second family to me. I don't know how to thank you for all you have done for me."

Before we could become too serious Harry said jokingly, "Well, I wasn't sure we could ever make a farmer out of you when I saw you attempt to milk that cow. She made me promise to never put her through that ordeal again!"

We all laughed as Ellen said. "At least Beverly tried; it takes time to develop the rhythm to milk cows."

"I don't know why you would want to go down to that smelly barn and milk cows anyway; I certainly wouldn't." Lorraine said in disdain.

"Bob was away that day, and I thought Harry could use some help," I replied, "but I guess milking cows is not my calling."

"If I recall you're not much of a janitor either," said Bob with a smile. "Maybe you should just stick to teaching."

Ellen had excused herself and was returning with a tray of warm apple pie, each slice topped by a piece of cheese. It had become my favorite dessert and, along with a cup of coffee, could serve as a complete meal for me.

I would never forget Ellen's smile as she placed the plate before me saying, "apple pie without cheese is like a hug without a squeeze."

My offer to help with the dishes was declined, as Ellen realized I hadn't finished packing. I thanked her for the delicious meal and all the others that I had enjoyed as a tenant in her home. She wiped her hands on her apron and gave me a hug saying "You are no tenant; you're a daughter to me."

It was nearly eleven o'clock when I put the last of my belongings into a box and went downstairs to prepare for bed. Harry and Ellen were in the living room reading and when I expressed my surprise Harry responded, "We are used to waiting until we know you are okay before we turn in. We were afraid that this might have been a hard day for you."

All I could do was thank them, as with tears in my eyes I said, "I'm just fine."

The following morning I awoke to the smell of coffee and bacon. I dressed hurriedly and went down to the kitchen where a big breakfast, complete with pancakes, was waiting.

Ellen and I had just taken our accustomed places at the table when Harry and Bob came in to join us.

Lorraine had finished her breakfast and was in the bathroom preparing for work. Bob, always the tease, knocked on the door and said in a loud voice, "Are there any snakes in there this morning, Rainey? You'd better check!"

While he washed his hands at the kitchen sink, she replied with exasperation, "I left it there for you." With that she bid us all goodbye and left for the day.

While we enjoyed our meal we recalled the day in the fall when there really was a snake in the bathroom. Lorraine had been inside, getting ready for work, when Ellen and I heard a blood curdling scream and Lorraine bounded out with a towel around her, screaming "There's a snake in there!"

In a few minutes Bob and Harry were on the scene and Lorraine, shaking from fright, pointed at the door and shouted, "There's a snake in there! Get it out! Get it out right now!"

Harry went into the room and came back with a medium sized garter snake, which he quickly deposited outside in the garden. After the bathroom was checked thoroughly and determined to be completely free of more reptiles, Lorraine went back inside and resumed her preparations for work.

The snake, it was determined, had come into the house in a basket of apples that the men had placed in the basement to keep cool. In search of a warmer place, it had evidently crawled up the cold air register and was enjoying its stay in the nice warm bathroom.

Our meal was delicious, especially the pancakes which Ellen made from her own secret recipe. "The Maple syrup is from our own trees," she said.

I recalled the morning in March when she had told me to be home early, as we were going to have supper at the sugar bush. I thought she was referring to a restaurant and I was surprised when I came home from school to find everyone dressed for outdoor weather and a wagon waiting to take us out to the woods.

Ellen had to explain that "sugar bush" was the name given to a stand of Maple trees from which sap was extracted to make syrup and candy.

She had prepared a meal of hot stew and some of her delicious baked goods, which were put on the wagon before we boarded for the trip across the pasture to the woods beyond.

Harry was already at the "shack" when we arrived. The barnlike building was filled with steam from big kettle of boiling sap which he was stirring; and the aroma of Maple syrup permeated the room.

Bob had left to empty the buckets that hung from spigots inserted into the Maple trees, while Lorraine and I helped Ellen lay out our picnic style meal. While Bob and Harry took turns at the caldron, we sat at a picnic table to eat the tasty meal that Ellen had prepared.

"You can make your own dessert," Harry had said as he handed small metal containers of hot maple syrup to Lorraine and me, directing us to take them outdoors and pour the contents on a spot of clean snow. In a few minutes we had created delicious Maple candy.

We had all worked together to clean the utensils and close down the "Sugar Bush" before boarding the wagon for the hayride back to the nice, warm farmhouse.

After the lengthy breakfast at which we shared fond memories of the past two years, Ellen surprised me with a gift of the Maple syrup that had been produced in the spring. "You can share it with your family if you wish," she said.

Before returning to their work, Bob and Harry carried my belongings to my big, waiting automobile. With most of my belongings in the back seat, there was room in the trunk for my desk which, padded and securely tied in place, was destined for Louie's summer apartment in Grand Rapids. There it would remain until we were ready to move to Naperville.

In short order the car was loaded and I was ready to head back to the city. "Now, come back to see us anytime," said Ellen; and I promised to do so, a promise I later found difficult to keep.

Then, with a few tears and hugs all around, I headed back to my other home in the city.

# GOUGEBURG SCHOOL 1952-1953

The new teacher: Beverly Haskins

Girl with a secret: Pamela Teesdale

Pals: Steven Powell, Jerry Manning,
and Allen Norman

Friends: Wayne Wainright
and Donna Dakens

An invitation: Patricia Becker

THE GRADUATES
Tom Teesdale and Leo Dakins
Ruth Knox and Patricia Becker

# GOUGEBURG SCHOOL 1953-1954

Swingers: Christine Long, Diana Davison, Sandra Teesdale, Lorene Dakins,
Jerry Manning, Judy Turner, Ruth Holden and Linda Dakins

Mothers Day Tea: Ellen Ray,
Ruth Holden

Christine Long, Craig Turner,
Steven Powell

Ronald Teesdale, at bat others (L-R)
Raymond Dimmick, Julie Holden,
Donald Manning, Earl Manning, and Carole Holden

1954 GRADUATES
Raymond Dimmick and Julie Holden

Edwards Brothers Malloy
Thorofare, NJ  USA
September 4, 2013